Simply Mary

Simply Mary

*Meditations on the Real Life of
the Mother of Christ*

James Prothero

RESOURCE *Publications* • Eugene, Oregon

SIMPLY MARY
Meditations on the Real Life of the Mother of Christ

Copyright © 2019 James Prothero. All rights reserved. Except for brief quotations in critical publications or reviews, no part of this book may be reproduced in any manner without prior written permission from the publisher. Write: Permissions, Wipf and Stock Publishers, 199 W. 8th Ave., Suite 3, Eugene, OR 97401.

Resource Publications
An Imprint of Wipf and Stock Publishers
199 W. 8th Ave., Suite 3
Eugene, OR 97401

www.wipfandstock.com

PAPERBACK ISBN: 978-1-7252-5125-0
HARDCOVER ISBN: 978-1-7252-5126-7
EBOOK ISBN: 978-1-7252-5127-4

Painting on cover, "The Annunciation" by Henry Ossawa Tanner

[Scripture quotations are from] Revised Standard Version of the Bible, New Oxford Annotated Bible, copyright © 2010 Oxford University Press. Used by permission. All rights reserved worldwide.

Manufactured in the U.S.A.   10/08/19

to
Fr Luke Dysinger, OSB
of St Andrew's Abbey, Valyermo

and

Fr Patrick Crerar
beloved Rector of St Clements by-the-Sea
Episcopal Church

How little people know who think that holiness is dull. When one meets the real thing . . . it is irresistible. If even 10% of the world's population had it, would not the whole world be converted and happy before a year's end?

—C.S. Lewis

We draw people to Christ not by loudly discrediting what they believe, by telling them how wrong they are and how right we are, but by showing them a light that is so lovely that they want with all their hearts to know the source of it.

— Madeleine L'Engle

Contents

Meditation One: A Surprise Visitor | 1

Meditation Two: Who is that Girl Anyway? | 4

Meditation Three: A Beginning | 19

Meditation Four: Whenever it Rains, it Pours | 32

Meditation Five: One Wild Christmas | 43

Meditation Six: Maryam's Sword | 51

Meditation Seven: Just When You Thought Nothing Would ever Change | 58

Meditation Eight: Another Lull | 67

Meditation Nine: The Storm Arrives | 72

Meditation Ten: Desperate Measures | 80

Meditation Eleven: The Very Worst that could Possibly Happen | 87

Meditation Twelve: The Surprises of *Adonai* | 97

Meditation Thirteen: Another Life | 101

Meditation Fourteen: Somewhere Over the Rainbow | 112

Bibliography | 121

Meditation One: A Surprise Visitor

I AM WRITING THIS book because I have been looking for it for years, but no one has dared to write it. I was always injudicious, so here I go. Certainly, I am not qualified, which is why I thought I should do it. Mary herself, by any measure of her time, was not qualified. It seems to be a good qualification to not be qualified. Ok, let me explain more clearly.

You don't have to believe me, but.... Lots of stories start that way, and belief is a complex thing. So you have the disclaimer. Ready? In 2005 one evening I was going to bed in my bedroom, in the house I still live in. At the foot of my bed I strongly sensed a human presence. I neither saw nor heard anything out of the ordinary. But I knew with an absolute certainty that Mary was standing there. There was no apparition as at Lourdes or Guadalupe. There was no message in particular. Beyond her presence, all I could sense was that she was interested in me. That stunned me. Interested in *me*? A high school English teacher in a southern California Mexican-American barrio? A no-reputation, part-time college professor in a massive herd of marginally-employed, part-time college professors? A nobody? Why? After about fifteen minutes, the presence faded.

About this time, I ceased to experience the symptoms of Wolf-Parkinson-White Syndrome, a heart arrhythmia which is more a nuisance than a threat, and a condition that had been with me at least since my middle twenties. Tachycardia was the most annoying part of it, though it can become dangerous in later life in combination with other problems. At my cardiologist's advice, I was treated for it by an arthroscopic surgery. Yet, when the specialist who performed the surgery found his way to my heart, there was no WPW to treat. He could not explain this when I talked to him later. My cardiologist was stumped. He'd seen the EKGs. It was there. An ER doctor and another cardiologist had seen it on the EKGs years before, and on vastly separate occasions. Only my cardiologist at the time and the specialist doing the surgery ever met each other of the four physicians who plainly read WPW on my EKGs. If this was a hallucination by my physicians, it was a mass-hallucination, and across time and space. Years later, I went for a third opinion. The fifth physician threw every WPW-associated test at me known to humankind, and found no evidence. He couldn't explain it. He shrugged. I was perplexed. My visit from Mary roughly corresponds with the time of the disappearance of my WPW. A healing? I can't be sure, but I can't help but wonder.

So you'll perhaps forgive me if from that time, I have had a burning curiosity about this girl from Nazareth. Frankly, I think her prayers did heal me, though I could not begin to prove it. Nevertheless, I want to explore Mary not only with the eyes of faith, but with an eye to what she really was and is, and not what we would project upon her. I'm hoping to look through windows and avoid mirrors. I was raised Presbyterian, spent fourteen years in the Catholic Church, and all of the rest of that time up till now, I have been Anglican, a member of the Episcopal Church. I will not be taking any denominational stance in the many-faceted Body of Christ. In fact, if you find this book infuriating, and you just might, it's because I will steadfastly refuse to take a stance that is either Protestant or Catholic, nor much anything else other than seeking the truth and why we are so taken with this peasant woman from first century Nazareth. But this woman came and visited me. And I'm totally stumped by that. I want to shed even just a little bit of light. Each of these diverse Christian traditions, as well as others, have added accretions and layers of myth and tradition over this simple village girl from Nazareth, much of it for the purpose of rendering her in our own image. In this book I'd like to see if we can get beneath those accretions to the real woman. Let's stop looking in mirrors and look out of windows instead.

And let me add clearly, I am not trying to find the "Historical Mary" in the same sense that a group of scholars some decades ago tried to find the "Historical Jesus" by eliminating all the supernatural elements in the story of Christ and reducing him to a deluded country preacher, a Jewish Buddha, whose teachings had been allegedly warped into modern Christianity. I am very devoted to the thought of C.S. Lewis, and agree with him that the impulse to try and take Christ and fit him into a materialistic denial of the supernatural is useless. Such a Christ would not interest anyone for long and would have no long-term relevance to any one of us. It is an Arian impulse and nothing new. If Christ is not the original ET, God visiting us, all matters of Christ, much less his mother, are vain and worthless. I write from a standpoint of faith. I have witnessed what science can't explain. I do not think that we can only believe that which we can scientifically prove. But that doesn't mean we have to believe without discernment. We are told to test the spirits.[1] That's what I intend to do here.

More delicately here, the road I'm going to travel will probably disappoint my Christian sisters and brothers on both sides of the Reformation. I am one with my Catholic and Orthodox siblings in that I have found Mary to be an active force of holiness in this dark world. For a "dead" woman, she is remarkably proactive. And I am keenly aware of her love and activity. But I will disappoint because I feel all that symbolic theological frosting we've added to Mary over the centuries, starting with the idea that she was ever-virgin in spite of the obvious reading of scripture, has made her distant and untouchable to many Christians. She doesn't share our pain, but instead floats in an ever-virgin bubble, hands folded and eyes closed, in endless bliss.

I will disappoint my Protestant sisters and brothers in that though I see Mary as a real woman who lived out all the pain of our existence, I think she was gifted with an unusual degree of holiness that no one can explain. And she has stayed engaged with us up till the present, though I can't explain how. But she's not just another woman. Both these views of Mary seem to me to miss the mark on opposite sides.

I want to find the real woman in the middle.

My Catholic experience teaches me that she has made herself known from time to time and place to place across the last two millennia in various locations. I'm not alone in being visited. Still, why visit me? Why would she do that? I thought myself then and even now as just one more person in this wide world, just one nobody among billions, beloved by friends and family perhaps, but beyond that no one significant. There was a line in the old Lone Ranger show that we used to watch as kids. When the Ranger and Tonto (a poor name choice for his friend, if you know Spanish) finished saving the day and rode off into the sunset, often some bystander would say, "Who was that masked man?" The answer always came, "That was the Loooooooonnnnnneeee Ranger."

Well, I have to ask: Who was that woman?

---

1. 1 John 4

Meditation Two: Who Is That Girl Anyway?

So, I suspect that I was healed by the prayers of Mary, but of course, there's no way I can prove that. But then that is always the pattern, is it not? God seems determined to flaunt our need to nail down objective, scientific proof. Revelations are made to those who have ears to hear. There is no mass campaign to prove God's miraculous powers. If there is any password into the Grace of God, it's not anything your lips could utter; it's having an open heart. If God has to put on a show for your insistent demand for proof, he's not going to bother. Jesus himself performed many signs, but never when they were demanded—only when they were unexpected.[1] Even as the Apostle Paul was seeing Christ on the Damascus road, none of his companions heard or saw anything they could make out.[2] God doesn't dance on command. He speaks to whom he will and when he does, we alone may be the only ones to hear.

As for Mary, Gabriel told her his news exactly in a way that would make everyone she cared about, her family and her fiancé, to doubt her. I can just imagine her thinking, "Just great. No one is going to believe me." I recently saw a painting from the Philadelphia Museum of Art, which I think the best Annunciation scene I've seen so far.(see the cover) It is by Henry Ossawa Tanner, and in it Mary is off to the right facing a blinding light to the left. She is dressed in simple, woolen robes. She is dark-skinned with coiling black hair. She is not particularly pretty in any current sense, nor does she have the Amish-girl, Caucasian look of Protestant Marys. All around her are the trappings of a poor woman's bedroom. Her face is troubled and uncertain, as we know from her own account of the event, conveyed in the Gospel of Luke, that she felt exactly troubled and uncertain. Her fingers are interlocked, as if to keep herself from trembling. She is leaning over, almost bowing before this supernatural presence. This is

---

1. Matthew 12:38,39
2. Acts 9:3-9

an artistic portrayal I could believe. *Why do we need Mary to be superhuman from day one?*

Mary obviously told someone, probably Luke himself, about the visit from the Angel Gabriel. In fact, the personal details in the Gospel of Luke not only in the Nativity story, but throughout, makes me suspect that Luke tapped her knowledge throughout the writing. They lack the vagueness of second or third-hand sources. Just think of Luke's line: "But Mary treasured all these things and pondered them in her heart."[3] I can hear Mary tell Luke, "I treasured these things in my heart and pondered them." How would he possibly know such a thing unless he'd either talked to Mary or someone to whom she'd given a very personal account? Treasuring and pondering are very specific and personal words. A second or third-hand source would most likely lapse into generalization and say something about how Christ's mother was affected by events. But we get specific words that ring with the personal admission. The line itself is acknowledgment of how personal this all was to her. Much of the other detail in Luke's Gospel has the ring of first-hand witness. I think there was a time and a place, perhaps in Ephesus, where Luke sat down with Mary and she told him what she remembered. And he used it in his Gospel. I've always thought of Luke's Gospel as The Gospel of Mary.

I said before that I was unqualified. But that's not strictly true. Certainly, though I took a few seminary classes, I'm not a Bible scholar, nor a theologian. By training I'm a literary critic. And that is how I will approach these texts—as texts that can be examined in the light of the times they were written. C.S. Lewis argues that one of the best indicators that the Gospel accounts are true are the amateurish way they are put together. They're too sloppy to have been anything but reporting by their amazed amateur authors. Those authors were clearly unqualified. But that's just the thing: God seems to love to select the unqualified. Look at Mary. Would any of us have picked a farmer's daughter from a nowhere corner of a conquered country? So my approach is twofold: I look at texts as reportage from which we can extrapolate subtle facts. And secondly, I insist that this reportage is about real people, who act like real people do. Thus, Luke knows far too much about things that only Mary would have known, and therefore I conclude that Luke at some point had a long talk with Mary. But enough of this. Back to Mary.

---

3. Luke 2:19

Let us return to the moment, as Tanner's painting portrays, Mary sat startled, and listened to this supernatural visitor. I suspect she didn't run right away and tell her mother and father, Joachim and Ana, their names by tradition. Would you have believed your teenage daughter if she'd broken into your room and announced she'd seen an angel and was pregnant with the Son of God? More likely you'd get up and check to see if she'd gotten into the liquor closet. Then, as now, we are so accustomed to think that the humdrum pattern of our existence is rock-bottom reality, that we are rather confused by the miraculous on the rare occasion it hits us in the face.

In looking for a really solid book on Mary, I have looked at the images that artists have projected over the centuries. Mostly, unlike Tanner, they have painted Mary in their own image, conforming to their own image of perfection. So, Mary is always portrayed as the ideal of attractiveness by the standards of the day and the culture, and invariably she is the same race as the artist, her Jewishness being brushed aside. Even the Protestant images of Mary-the-Amish-girl make her sleepy and content, but always tremendously pretty and white.

And I could see all around me the representations of Mary in art. She is always calm. Most of the time she is looking away, or simply up at the sky. In some of the older Greek icons, she looks you straight in the eyes with a passionless, poker-face, like she just beat your full house with a straight flush. She is also always decked out either puritanically neat and trim—the way Protestants prefer to visualize her—or she is covered with gold and jewels, any one single gem of which would be worth more than all the wealth in her village, Nazareth. This is the way Catholics and the Orthodox like to see her. The puritanical, Protestant Mary always looks like a good girl, and here in America, her face tones are lightened and her hair is often shaded brown, in order to make her seem like a white girl.

However, European art beat us Americans to presenting Mary as a very white, European-looking girl, as in the many portraits of her as Madonna and Child. In them she most often looks a little sleepy, very unworried and relaxed, or at least I believe that to have been the artist's intention. I am a painter myself and I would never take on the challenge of trying to paint Mary. For how do you portray in the muscles of the face the quality of spiritual intensity? Certain shameless wags have said of the Renaissance pictures of the Virgin Mary that she looked like she had a bad case of gas more than she looked spiritual. I am afraid I can quite see their point. The

Protestant Virgin Marys are no better; they tend to look bored or a little sleepy, like they were on sedatives.

In Latin America, she is Our Lady of Guadalupe and her selling point was that she appeared like a First Nations young woman, a Native American girl. This too seems a projection. But of all the projections out there, this one must be closer to the truth. A dark-skinned, black-haired Palestinian girl would be my model were I to dare to paint Mary. Native American is close, though the facial bone structure is different between Native America and the Middle East.

What strikes me in all of this is how much when we think we're looking through a window at something outside of us, we unconsciously turn that window into a mirror, so that what we see outside of us is more likely just . . . us.

Mary I take to have been, and to still be a woman who prefers to peer through clean windows and shows no interest in mirrors.

Scott Hahn's book *Hail Holy Queen* was very helpful, but his agenda was to explain to Protestants why Catholics were so in love with the Virgin Mary. Sadly, it wasn't what I was looking for. Then I thought I'd found the book on Mary that I needed. It was *Mary: A Flesh-and-Blood Biography of the Virgin Mother* by Lesley Hazleton. Hazleton started off so well, acquainting the reader with the everyday life of a girl in Galilee in the first century. She had obviously done some real research, and was familiar with Israel and the history of the area. But Hazleton wrote from the perspective of the Jewish faith, and this only faintly. She explained how our name for Mary comes from the Hebrew name, Maryam, a form of Miriam, a name possibly meaning "bitterness". Our current "Mary" is a lift of the name as it appears in two forms in the New Testament Greek, either "Maryam" or "Maria."

But back to Hazleton, what began well, turned into a speculation of how Maryam of Nazareth really was a misunderstood herbal healer who taught herbal healing to her son, so that he could perform healings that others considered miracles. In the end, Hazleton's Mary is a New-Age spiritual pilgrim. Hazleton turns another window turned into a mirror. I say this meaning no disrespect to our Jewish brothers and sisters. And if Jews are skeptical of Christ, it may have something to do with the appalling and homicidal way Christians have treated them over the last few centuries. The Holocaust was merely the frosting on a deadly cake of centuries of persecution. G.K. Chesterton said that the biggest argument against Christianity is Christians. For Jews, this has been tragically and lethally true for a very long time.

And it is even sadder when we think that this gilded Catholic or Orthodox Madonna, or this puritanical, white-skinned, virgin Mother of Protestant tradition, was and is actually a Jewish girl. Her son was and is still Jewish too. I have since found other books that have helped me. Sally Cunneen's *A Search for Mary: The Woman and the Symbol* was almost the book I needed. It provides much useful and objective information. It lacked but one thing: it was not written from a standpoint of faith.

But even so, I wasn't sure *why* Hazleton was writing. If Jesus of Nazareth, Jeshua of Nazareth if you will, was not the Messiah, the Christ, then, as C.S. Lewis has argued, he was a lunatic, or a fantastically gifted con-man. In either case, if Maryam of Nazareth is not the Mother of Christ, why should we have any interest in her at all? Why bother? Do we normally study the mothers of lunatics and con-men?

It is when the miraculous touches a rude, simple farm-girl, making her the Mother of God Incarnate, that we first are intrigued. Her? That simple country-bumpkin with the straw in her uncombed, long, straight black hair? Her? Still smelling like the dung she just shoveled out of the stalls? Not Maryam! She's destined for some working man's wife, driving away whatever youthful beauty she might possess with the brutal life of woman's work in a poor agricultural village, popping out babies until childbirth or disease catch her and her life flutters out like a snuffed candle.

But I have to assume that there was a quality in this dark-skinned girl raking out the stalls that the Creator of the Universe, the God of Israel found compelling, that he chose her from all the young women ever born to humankind across all the millennia. To God, she was and is one women in trillions. To be chosen the vehicle by which the Creator invaded his own creation—the thought is beyond my grasp. But unlike Hazleton, I must write from a standpoint of faith. Otherwise, why bother? If you want a cold, scientific, or even New Age, or perhaps militant-feminist Mary, a "Historical Mary," who can explain-away all the miraculous elements, Hazleton's book awaits you. You can stop reading this book right now. If you just want responsible information, I recommend Cunneen's book. I have been touched by miracle. I have to write from that place.

But as I said, I have to assume that there was a quality in this dark-skinned girl that Almighty God chose. What would it look like? I dare not try to paint it. I'm not sure I could improve on the Italian Renaissance and their gassy Madonnas, nor our current crop of Protestant, sedated Marys. But I do suspect that it would be surprising to us, not what we would expect. If we walked into a room with Jesus' family, un-introduced, we probably couldn't pick her out. We'd either be looking for the Protestant Virgin, whom to our minds would look faintly Amish, or the Catholic and Orthodox Blessed Virgin, who would overwhelm everyone in the room with her golden glow and opulent clothes. We'd probably all miss the dark girl in the corner, talking to her friends, wearing plain, undyed woolen robes. I like her in blue, as all the pictures portray, but dye was for rich people—poor people like Mary's family used their money to buy food, and there was never enough for that. Whatever they might spare financially was sucked up by Roman taxes. Rich girls wore dyed robes. If the Virgin Mary ever had blue robes, it was and is only in Heaven. Perhaps Mary is a little distracted, or perhaps looking at all the people in the room with love, but at the same time all too aware of what makes a small town odious: the petty jealousies, the gossip, and the pride. There would be a sadness in her eye to see this all around her. She would not stand out, nor be primly puritanical. She would just be, to our eyes, yet another poor young woman among her family.

So, imagine how much faith it took for her to say yes to the angel, knowing full well that an unwed mother-to-be might be stoned by those who follow rules without love. It would mean she would have to stand out for once. And I suspect she was more of an introvert. This was cruelly hard for her, but she took it on. I think you would see determination in her face. You may not notice her, but you'd think twice about messing with her. Intensity, not sleepiness or gassiness is the quality that emanates from her. Her son "set his face" to go to Jerusalem, crucifixion and death.[4] We have to think, especially with the Spirit of God for a father, that the genetic side of Our Lord came from Mary. I tend to think that she too could "set her face" to do something, including risk her life to assent to be an unwed mother for God. I think she was—and still is, very formidable. But how to portray that in art without making her look like she just missed her bus and was ticked off about it? Well, that's the hard part. Human emotions are many and varied and telling a story in paint by a face could have many interpretations. If we had spent any time with Mary during her life here, I think we would find that she surprised us at every turn; we would feel that we could never get to the bottom of her. And we'd be right.

Why do we need Mary to be superhuman from day one?

Why do we need Mary to be superhuman from day one? And here I immediately come perilously close to the minefield of Protestant versus

---

4. Luke 9:51

Catholic. Protestant artists, writers, and theologians view Mary as a mere woman, a sinner like the rest of us, though probably better than most, chosen to bear the Son of God. Catholics by official dogma, hold Mary to have been "immaculately conceived", without sin, and assumed into Heaven at death. The Orthodox agree with them. Much of that gassy Renaissance art was meant to portray a perfect, superhuman, and blonde-north-Italian Mary. And even though my Protestant friends do not hold to the concept of immaculate conception, they still portray her as patient, silent, and supportive of her son. I don't wish to even try to weigh in on one side or another in this issue. I would rather explore why we have such a fissure in world Christianity over a peasant girl from Nazareth, and what we do actually know or can surmise.

But I have to get back to my question: why do we need Mary to be superhuman from day one? The question may seem to be pointed squarely at Catholics, but the Protestant Mary is rather super in her own different way. The Protestant problem with the Catholic veneration of Mary, and "Mariology" is that they fear it is heresy, if not idolatry. They believe that Catholics have made Mary the fourth member of the Trinity, a goddess. Certainly, all the Orthodox and Catholic art with a glowing, gilded Virgin Mary, heaped up with jewels leaves this impression on Protestants, which may explain why they always go out of their way to portray her in very modest and plain first-century costume. I would say the Protestant portrayals were more accurate if they didn't try so hard to make Mary look Caucasian. In either case, we're taking a country girl from Nazareth and turning her into something far more. But I don't mean to laugh at either my Catholic, Protestant, nor Orthodox sisters and brothers. I think the answer is that we all sense there is something special to this girl, beyond just who her son is. And our art reflects our understanding. If Catholic and Orthodox Marys are glowing and jewel-bedecked, it is merely the clumsy way of the artist trying to portray what paint can never portray, the inner qualities of the woman. With my Protestant sisters and brothers, I have to hold that Mary was no goddess. And the Catholic and Orthodox churches teach that she's not, even if in some less developed parts of the world, syncretism has set in, and festivals once held for goddesses are now held for the Virgin Mary. It seems to me that we are all grasping after something, in very awkward ways that reflect our own cultures more than we'd like to admit. We are all trying to grasp the something special in this unremarkable peasant girl. It's a puzzle.

MEDITATION TWO: WHO IS THAT GIRL ANYWAY?

And the biggest piece of the puzzle is that she won't leave us alone.

But more on that point in separate chapters. In the meanwhile, what do we know or think we know about her life?

The *Protevangelium of James* and other biographies

Somewhere around 145 CE someone, pretending to be the James who wrote the New Testament letter, wrote the *Gospel of James*. It contains a story of Jesus's youth and before that, Mary's. Most of what it claims is hard to believe, not because I distrust the supernatural, but because it doesn't ring true. Test the spirits. In fact, some elements are so incredible and so out of consonance with the real Gospel, that it reads like somebody's comic satire. In this writing, Mary is born and raised exactly like Samuel in the Old Testament. She is the result of the prayers of a barren mother. She is presented at the Temple at age 3 and grows up a temple virgin. Though the united church of the first millennium condemned this book as not credible, its general pattern found its way into the writings of other mystics over the centuries on Mary. Maximus the Confessor writes a similar glowing story of a Mary who is superhuman and unnaturally pious. A visionary nun named Catherine of Emmerich did much the same in the Middle Ages. In all these stories, Mary is far beyond human. She spends all her time in meditation and prayer, unmoving, hands palm together, eyes closed, almost a perfect female Buddha. One wonders if she moved to eat, to relieve herself. Did she bother to breathe? I mean no irreverence, but I cannot believe in such a person. That is a clumsy cartoon of holiness, not holiness itself.

One version has her not only a Temple virgin, but living in the Holy of Holies, that place in the Temple where only the High Priest went, and him only once a year. I understand the symbolism in this: God was extremely present in the Holy of Holies and in the womb of Mary. I still don't think Jewish priests are going to let a small girl into the Holy of Holies, far beyond the Court of Women, never mind that she's not even a priest, but of the family of David, and therefore of the tribe of Judah, and not Levi, as priests were.

For anyone who is a skeptic, these tales are not helpful, for it would be easy to conclude by looking at these that the Gospel itself was the fabrication of pious fantasy and extremism. Even the most basic research shows it up. One internet site I easily found cast some interesting light on the whole idea of Mary being raised in the Temple:

> Did the Herodian Temple have virgins? The answer is almost certainly *no*. The only real support for Jewish temple virgins is found in Roman Catholic writings in support of the Catholic doctrine of the perpetual virginity of Mary. This doctrine has no basis in the canonical scriptures, but only in non-canonical early writings, most of which were influenced or produced by the Essenes and similar mystical and ascetic quasi-Christians sects that existed in the first few centuries of the Christian era. Jewish scholars and historians, by contrast, give a definitive "no" to the question of whether there were Jewish temple virgins.

But included in this was something I thought far more important.

> Unlike in Catholicism, in Judaism marriage is considered the most holy state, pursuant to the first commandment of God given in the Hebrew Bible: "Be fruitful and multiply, and fill the earth, and subdue it" (Genesis 1:28). In Judaism[,] celibacy is frowned upon and even considered sinful. To have consecrated virgins at the Temple would violate Jewish sacred law and custom. No *Jewish* writings, ancient or modern, provide any support for the idea that there were temple virgins at the Temple in Jerusalem. (StackExchange: Christianity)

And here I am going to step squarely into the minefield. Both the Catholic Church and the Orthodox Church have come down believing that Mary was ever-virgin, and between them they constitute the vast majority of the world's Christians. Protestants doubt this, probably because part of the Protestant revolution was a rejection of the perpetual celibacy of priests and monastics, modeled in part on this idea that the Mother of God in her excessive purity, was ever-virgin.

And this goes back to my first question: why do we need Mary to be superhuman?

The answer, I submit, is both simple and intrinsically confused. We deck Mary with gold and diamonds, and also we contemplate theological formulas like immaculately conceived, and ever-virgin, for the same reason. We know no other way to paint a quality we cannot easily grasp in words.

Holiness.

Wait, says the reader. Are you telling me she was sinless all her life? Are you coming down on the side of immaculate conception and ever-virginity? Are you, O writer, siding with the Catholics and the Orthodox against the Protestants? Minefield again.

No, I'm not. I have left my jury out on those questions, mainly because though I point out the words and images we wrap around Mary, and their weakness, I doubt I'm any better or wiser, that I can substitute any better. I want to clarify, not just replace the images. What I do hold is that something—holy—I'm sorry, but there just isn't any other word that will do; something holy hangs about her both in the past and the present. And I think she had this quality, though I doubt the formulas of immaculate conception and ever-virginity. I have to wonder if the belief in perpetual virginity isn't theologically not too different from the work of those Italian Renaissance painters who in their quest for portraying beauty and spiritual depth, ended up making Mary look northern-Italian, blond, and a bit gassy. We exaggerate, as the artists did, to portray something we can't quite name. For some people, understanding how Mary is so pro-active in our lives needs her to be rather unique. After all, as a feminist might point out, a woman who is celibate is a woman who is not ruled by a man. Even our feminine super-heroes, like Wonder Woman, stay unattached. And those first century Christians were often Greeks who were used to very moral and self-possessed goddesses, like Artemis and Athene, being virgins. Virginity was a symbol of feminine strength and independence.

I hope to avoid the trap of taking the Protestant or the Catholic/Orthodox point of view myself, and the only way I can do that is to only claim to know what I can extrapolate from what we do know, or to talk of what others have witnessed.

Going back to the *Gospel of James* that I mentioned above, it is rife with absurdities that smack of Manichaee and Gnostic thought: Ana and Joachim conceive Mary at a distance of many miles, as Joachim has gone out into the desert for 40 days to pray about his childlessness. (Some later accounts have the conception as a result of the couple kissing). When Mary finally does give birth to the Lord Jesus, Joseph is away looking for a midwife, and when he returns the baby Jesus is lying there, clean as a whistle, no blood or amniotic fluid around, and Mary has birthed him without pain and miraculously teleported him out of her womb. Perhaps she called up to the Enterprise and had Scotty beam Jesus out of the womb. I know that sounds absurd, but no more absurd than the *Gospel of James* itself. It reads on one hand as if it were a ribald satire written by Monty Python, and on the other hand like the tale of a goddess who hovers above human suffering, untouched. And the reason for all this absurdity is the silly conviction that Mary *must* remain a virgin at all costs. The Manichaee/Gnostic sentiment is so strong in this ancient document that we are told that after the birth, Mary was "intact." In plain language, the birth of her son had not split her hymen and it is implied that nothing ever, ever did.

None of this makes any sense at all except for the Manichaee and Gnostic concept, the primitive human concept that sex and spiritual power are mutually exclusive. The Apostle Paul didn't believe it.[5]

That's a human idea.

It's not God's idea.

Which is why I don't see why Mary cannot have been sexually active with her husband after Jesus' birth and still have an aura of holiness about her. Why does she *need* to be ever-virgin, except for the notion that sex saps spiritual power? And that brings me to the second reason. As the quote above says, for the Jews, the holiest state was matrimony. This would have been Mary's mindset. Why should she try to remain a virgin in a married household? And third, in the Jewish understanding of the time, not only the marriage feast, but the sexual consummation were necessary for a marriage to have taken place. I can understand Joseph waiting till Mary was no longer pregnant, but what reason would he have to wait after that? To be called her 'husband' as scripture does, is to say that they were man and wife in the flesh, given the Jewish meaning of the word.

It was Roman Empire era sect called the Manichaees who thought lifelong virginity equaled holiness. It was also a Gnostic idea, and they got it from the Docetists, who believed Jesus was too holy to ever have had human flesh. All these groups thought that the human body, and therefore sex, were inherently evil, while the spiritual side was inherently good. And though the Roman Catholic and Orthodox churches officially declare sex within marriage to be a good and holy thing, they both have echoes of the Manichaee/Gnostic beliefs, mainly in the stories of the saints, who not only have sexual self-control, a long-standing Christian virtue, but are totally free of all sexuality. Thus, we hear of this or that saint, followed by "virgin", as if it was a credit to them that they did not commit the sin of having sex.

It is a curious thing how this contradiction in church teaching versus popular perception arose. The rise of monasticism led to the logical mistake that celibacy was a holier state. So as Mary receives more and more attention with the theological debates of the 300s and 400s, Mary has to be ever-virgin in order to have been holy enough to be the mother of Christ at all. More than this, a form of Christianity that believed that Jesus was just a man, son

---

5. 1 Corinthians 7:5

of Joseph and Mary, called "Arianism", became very popular for a while, and threatened to drown "catholic" Christianity, that is Christianity as we know it today. In those hot debates it was either Mary was never a virgin or forever a virgin. All nuance was dismissed and people faced off on extreme sides of the issue. Anger makes people simplify and oppose.

The Middle Ages in many cases moved rituals that had once been worship of pagan virgin goddesses, almost unchanged into veneration of Mary. That's how we got the glowing Madonna and we lost the country girl from Nazareth. Though I should point out that Protestants with their puritanism didn't do a whole lot better when it came to avoiding the Manichaee belief in the wickedness of human flesh and the embrace of an extreme asceticism.

I agree with the Jewish position quoted above: God made married partners to join in fleshly union and declared it good. Even in 1 Corinthians 7 Paul calls believers to whatever life God has ordained for them, celibate or family. Neither is superior nor inferior—just different. Yes, one might dedicate oneself to God and never marry, as monks and nuns do. But that is about focusing one's life, not about sex being somehow evil or spiritually inferior. Too many people fail to see this distinction. And making Mary of Nazareth into some super-virgin with virgin super-spiritual-powers is a blurring of the truth. A think our Protestant sisters and brothers have a point: we do the truth and Mary herself no favors by effectively making her a goddess.

But on the Other Hand . . . .

She is the *Theotokos,* the God-bearer. There is no getting away from that. The Orthodox, like their Catholic sisters and brothers, stand by this, as they do her ever-virginity. So, once again, I'm dancing here in double-heresy, from both sides of my faith. I must be one of those crazy Anglicans.

Part of the Protestant problem with this is the rejection of asking prayers of the dead who are with Christ, that is, the saints. Their rejection of this is understandable, given how badly this belief was abused by the time of the Renaissance. Phony saint's relics were a major market in the Middle Ages, as Chaucer likes to satirize in his *Canterbury Tales.* And there are still places in the world where pagan festivals have been turned into saints' festivals with very little difference. For some peoples of the world, the saints are seen to be minor gods, and this Protestants find offensive. I don't blame them. But it may be another case in history (and there are many) where we have thrown the baby out with the bathwater. What the Catholic and Orthodox churches actually teach is that those who have gone to be with the Lord, through the medium of the Holy Spirit, can still pray for us. This belief is known as "the Communion of Saints." And just as I might ask for the prayers of someone I feel is close to God in preference, so the saints are close to God. You can argue with it, but if you take the time to talk to enough people who do it, like my heart healing, it is a mystery why so many prayers have been answered this way.

And face it, to Bernadette at Lourdes, Mary said, "I am the immaculate conception." I don't see why she needs to be, but then most things God does I cannot claim to understand. If I'm going to credit my small visitation, I can hardly throw rocks at Bernadette. As I said above, I wonder if some of our theological language like "immaculate conception" really is a near miss or a symbol for the reality. I have little problem with the immaculate part; what I can't accept is the conception part. This immaculately conceived, ever-virgin vision of Mary is of a detached woman, if she's really a woman in any sense that we know, born perfect, living in meditative bliss, at least if the paintings are to be believed, giving birth by teleportation and then topping it all off with turning her husband's home into a convent for her and a monastery for him. And she does this in the face of all the Jewish teaching she's grown up with, that a husband and wife should become one flesh.

I cannot believe she was and is that detached. And I cannot believe that for at least two reasons. First, she was promised a sword in her soul. She did not have an easy life. And second, like many who have experienced great pain and tragedy, her empathy for those who are poor and suffering is born of her own poverty and suffering. The book of Hebrews says of her son: "Although he was a Son, he learned obedience from what he suffered."[6] If the eternal Son of God had to learn obedience from suffering, why should his mother, Mary, escape the common suffering of humanity and live on a cloud of perfection? These things don't happen abra-cadabra Poof! and all of a sudden Mary knows about empathy. Her Son, our Lord, was not spared pain, nor did he seek to avoid it. Why should she float effortlessly above the dirt and blood and hunger? Some people think that's what holiness looks like. But we should know better. Her son, our Lord, exhibited holiness by feeding the hungry and healing the sick, not by sitting in some permanent, painless meditative state. As did he, so I have to believe, so did she.

6. Hebrews 5:8

So I believe Mary's vast empathy, which is a common element in all her later appearances, came the hard way. I believe she became immaculate, but the way most of us grow, through pain. Mary paid her dues and it became holiness for her. This is the grace she was given, the grace that fills her. And if she likes to appear these days to poor children and children out watching flocks, that may have something to do with Mary the little poor girl in the hills around Nazareth, watching flocks. Those are her kind of people. And Simeon promised that a sword would pierce her heart and soul. But I believe this was more than witnessing the horrible execution of her son; this was all her life. Still, still, I am convinced that an unusual grace was and is granted to her, who knows, perhaps at birth. And she doesn't need to be ever-virgin for this to be true.

In the end, I'm one of those crazy Anglicans, asking questions and reluctant to queue up in anyone's pre-set line of march. So, if you will, bear with me. I want to do what I hoped Hazleton and Cunneen had done: through the eyes of faith, I want to go through the life of Mary, minus all the unbelievable, gassy spirituality of writers like Catherine of Emmerich and Maximus, and really explore who this first-century peasant woman had to be from what we know, and how that expanded into the woman who just doesn't seem to want to leave us alone, and hasn't taken her death as a halt on her activity on this small planet. I hope that in doing so, those who have rejected her in their minds, might find a way to see her at work in the world without all that imagery and theology that make her look like some disconnected goddess, and instead see her as a woman, and all that comes with being a woman.

I realize this is a rather odd sort of biography, which is why these are meditations, and not a claim to know that everything I'm about to propose is historical fact. For one thing, most of my assertions are speculation based on what we do know, and I do not pretend they are more. Except for Herod's land grab, most of this cannot be proven from the written record, apart from the Bible. But I am extrapolating from two sources. First, we know much about the personality of Mary's son, the Son of God. And since all his human DNA came from Mary, I think we can assume much of his behavior came from her as well. As a father myself, I have seen proof in my daughter that some behavior is genetic. So I am assuming that Jesus acted a whole lot like his mother. The second thing that makes this odd is that I am not trying to portray too many day-to-day events. Sholem Asch has written a biographical novel, titled *Mary*, but neither is that what

I'm trying to do here. I am taking points from what we know of history and archaeology, and what we know of Jesus, and the "mere Christianity" as Lewis called it, the common beliefs of all the branches of the church, and trying to find the real woman there, who lives now in Heaven and seems so very active in our world. Throw the "feminist" word at me if you like, but women are equal to men, (on the occasions when they're not superior) in spite of the convictions of our ancestors that they were not, and Mary has shown herself to be an incredible and triumphant *woman*. Got that? Woman. Not a glowing female Buddha or a subservient and silent kitchen-worker-good-girl. Not Northern-Italian nor Amish. Jewish. Woman. Dark-skinned. Poor. Incredible. Woman.

I want to write about Mary from a vantage point of faith, without the symbolic hyperbole that makes her less a real woman and more a glowing, feminine Buddha. If Mary is first among women, first, she was and is, a woman.

Meditation Three: A Beginning

So Mary was and is a woman, born poor, in an agricultural village far from the heart of a Judaism centered around Jerusalem. Recent archaeological digs in Nazareth indicate that during the first century the population was a mix of Jewish and non-Jewish people, so Mary grew up not only amongst her own people, but among Gentiles. We don't know her father's profession, if he was named Joachim. There is good reason to believe his name was actually "Heli" and he was descended from David, if we believe that the genealogy in the Gospel of Luke is actually Mary's. I'm going to go with that assumption for the purposes of this meditation. There's a good chance that Heli's profession was farming and that the first home she knew was a farmhouse on the edge of town. The Bible tells us that she was of the line of David, the tribe of Judah, even though Galilee was the territory of the tribe of Naphtali. But most of those northern tribes had been deported by the Assyrians centuries back and even during the time of the Maccabees, those Jews still in Galilee were pulled out. Apparently, they didn't all pull out. And perhaps, searching for affordable land to farm, other Jews from the surviving tribe of Judah in the south had wandered north and moved into towns around the Sea of Galilee, and further inland as well. The fact that both Joseph and Mary claimed descent from David indicates that Jews from the south, of the principle surviving tribe of Judah, were populating Galilee. Certainly, there were other survivors, and Hazleton makes an error here when she presents Mary's family as northerners who didn't trust those southern Jews. Certainly, there was a small distinction in customs and language. We know from the Gospel, when Peter is denying Christ, that he had a Galilean accent that gave him away. But Jesus and Peter, though Galileans, were still Jews, and mostly likely, Jesus, Peter and the rest of the Galilean disciples were from southern stock originally.

But Hazleton confuses Mary's people with the Samaritans, who were survivors of the destroyed northern tribes, mixed in with Gentile stock. The Samaritans still exist today, a small group in the State of Israel, insisting on their worship away from Jerusalem and seeing themselves as much part of ancient Israel as their more populous relatives who are descended from the tribes of Judah, Benjamin, and to some degree, Levi, and Simeon. Now, as then, Israeli Jews consider Samaritans as half-breeds. The DNA evidence supports their claim to being purer blood Jewish, as they've always claimed. But the dwindling numbers of the Samaritans today make the sort of antagonism known in Jesus' time irrelevant. Mary's family was up from the south. They were no Samaritans—though it is interesting that Mary's son had no problem talking freely to Samaritans.

Let's be like Scrooge and the ghosts of Christmas, and invisibly visit Mary's home. Heli—if that is his name—is there, wringing his hands in the dark of the sleeping room he shares with Ana, for other than the light from the fire and the light through the door, the windows are narrow and high up on the wall beneath the eaves to keep in heat or cool and keep out smells in this mud-and-stone house, which would look to American eyes like a primitive adobe house. The rooms are gathered around a central courtyard, fenced off by a mud-and-stone wall around the perimeter. The roof is mud, sticks, and rushes. The floor is dirt. Ana, Heli's wife, is on a pallet bed in the corner attended by two midwives, women of the village of Nazareth. They tell Heli to go outside, which he does. This is woman's work. Men are worse than useless at a birthing.

And I'm reminded of all the Christmas cards I've seen picturing Mary having just given birth to Jesus in clean, blue robes, looking peaceful. This is an echo of the Manichaee and Gnostic concept that Jesus was cleanly teleported out of Mary's womb and left her hymen intact. I cannot say just how much I find that unbelievable. I believe that just as her son experienced the pain and dirt and hard aches of human life, so was Mary exposed to these things. If pain and dirt and frustration were allowed to visit the Son of God, surely his mother wasn't spared them.

So years later, Mary gave birth like any other woman—in incredible pain that no male has the ability to stand. Tests have been done recently on men with technology which allows them to experience the pain of childbirth. And the men were given a kill switch when they couldn't stand it anymore. So far, no man has made it all the way through the test. Women are provably far better at taking pain than men.

Childbirth, even today, in the 21st century, with modern medicine, is noisy, painful, and very sloppy, with blood and amniotic fluid flowing everywhere. In the first century it was done in sanitary conditions that were appalling. Women often did not survive it, either because the birth was too difficult, or they contracted infection in the process, what used to be called "puerperal fever", and died shortly after giving birth. Caesarian section was an option, but it invariably killed the woman. To be a wife was to be in constant risk of pregnancy, and risking death with every childbirth. Women of this era were saddened and shamed if they were infertile and couldn't give birth—at least that's what the stories tell. With disease and hunger and war bringing death so frequently, the insurance that the family would continue was to have as many children as needed to help on the farm, and maybe a couple of spares. This was done in hope that enough of them would survive to adulthood and become the caregivers for one's final years. But I often wonder how many infertile women of the time secretly rejoiced in the realization that they would not risk childbirth and death.

There is a tradition amongst the Orthodox that the reason Jesus had brothers and sisters was that Mary was Joseph's second wife. Given how often women died in childbirth, this is fully believable. Men often went through three wives in a lifetime and never divorced.

But Ana pulls through the birth, with only the usual amount of screaming, while Heli paces outside in his courtyard and is comforted by other men of the village standing about to offer support. It would have been a long vigil; if Ana took the average time, she was in agony for eighteen hours. Yet, the midwives know their job and the baby wails into the afternoon air. The umbilical is cut. The afterbirth is evacuated. Hopefully, the midwives didn't accidentally infect Ana's womb. We won't know for possibly a few weeks, which is the amount of time that Puerperal Fever needs to take hold and kill a woman. Ana is cleaned up and the soiled and soggy, bloody woolen sheets that were under Ana are disposed of. Like in most pre-industrial societies, women's blood frightens men. Under Jewish law, they were ritually polluted. The woolens will be burned as ritually unclean. The women will have to undergo a ritual bath after the business is done. Ana and the child will be ritually unclean for two weeks. Heli can't hold his new daughter till then or risk being ritually unclean himself. And Ana should make a cleansing offering in the Jerusalem temple, an expensive journey, but one demanded by the law. I suspect that she and many poor women merely took a ritual bath and left the trip to Jerusalem for another time when they could afford it.

The midwife comes out to Heli. "You have a daughter, Heli. She is healthy."

Lusty wailing from inside the house confirms the midwife's account. Heli rushes in to meet his newest daughter. We are never told whether or not Mary had siblings. The fantastic tales make Ana barren except for Mary. It is possible that she was an only child. But the odds are that she had siblings, just because women became pregnant so often. It was considered their duty to do so. So it is very possible several brothers and sisters crowded into the space around their father to meet their new sister. Or perhaps she was the first-born. Her fiery confidence later in life makes me suspect that she was a first-born.

"What will we call her?" he asks.

"I will name her for the sister of Moses, Miriam," Ana replies. And so it is. Ana is illiterate and has never read the Torah and the story of Moses. But it is read every Shabat in the synagogue, and she knows it by heart. But the old stories are in Hebrew, a language they know vaguely, and Heli and his family speak the language of the ancient conquerors, Aramaic. We cannot know what vowels they pronounced. Aramaic is still a living language, but languages change over two-thousand years. We don't know what the name the family called her sounded like. The question of how Mary spelled her name is irrelevant. The answer is that she grew up illiterate and never once spelled it. The New Testament gives it as Maryam, and sometimes Maria, the Latin variation. I doubt there was much difference in pronouncing Maryam and Miriam.

As Maryam grows up, she begins to know the world. Since in a world of no birth control and the need for children to work a farm is the most likely scenario, I will go with my assumption that she is the eldest. Heli and Ana need sons to help work the farm and provide for their old age, presuming they live long enough to have one. Around her second and fourth years, two brothers are born and of course, her status as eldest is now irrelevant, because she is a girl. Let us call them Jacob and Jeremiah. For though she is older, they are boys, helping their father in the fields, while Maryam aids her mother in the home. But farm life is too tough for a strict definition of male and female work to hold forever. There are times when Jacob and Jeremiah are with Heli in the fields and Mary rakes out the stalls for the goats and sheep, or the cattle. Work is work and has to be done.

Given the odds, it's quite possible that the birth of the second son was more than Ana could survive. A difficult birth, or perhaps an infection, or even both, claim her life at the birth of Jeremiah. I picture Maryam, now lady of the house at age seven, while her brothers and father labor in the fields. Heli is alone without Ana, and too poor to consider attracting another wife. Plus, another tragedy has befallen Heli. But more on that in a bit. First, let's look outside in the farmyard and see if we can find Maryam. When she's not working the kitchen fire or cleaning, she's herding the goats, sheep, and any cattle. Her aunt Rachel, her mother's sister, and her cousin Dvorah come over frequently and help her with the baking and sweeping. Rachel teaches her carding and weaving of wool, and soon she is making the family's clothes in addition to feeding them and cleaning the home. As Maryam grows in ability, Aunt Rachel comes over less and then not at all. By age nine, Maryam manages the house for her father and brothers all on her own, leaving her little time to be a child.

From Scott Korb's excellent book, *Life in Year One*, we learn that Herod Antipas, effectively the Roman-backed king of Galilee, instituted a program in the first century where his wealthy friends bought up farm lands and pushed sustenance farmers like Heli off their lands. Using something akin to eminent domain, farmers were forced to sell out to King Herod's cronies, and then be hired for small wages as tenant farmers to work what had once been theirs. It was a clear moving of wealth in vast amounts into the hands of a few of Herod's wealthy friends, who now became great land-owners, and farming became what we now call agribusiness. Talk about plans to create economic inequality and the rule of the 1%. Nazareth was but three miles from Herod's Romanized capital at Sepphoris. There's no way that Nazareth would be spared the new land policies, being so close. The record shows that Herod Antipas expropriated all but three percent of Galilean farm land this way. And that means, unless Heli was an artisan/mason/carpenter like his future son-in-law, Joseph, there's a 97% chance he got caught up in the land-grab.[1]

I can see Mary standing hurt and bewildered in the courtyard of her father's house, her brothers silently standing next to her, as the agent of the king, one Lucius, in fine clothes, backed by two heavily-armed soldiers to make sure everything goes smoothly, shoves a small bag of coins into Heli's hand, explaining that Heli is now his employee and tenant. Mary's family goes from growing their own food to having to live by a handful of coins from month to month, risking hunger even as the fields around their house are bursting with plenty. And then I think of the words:

---

1. Korb, *Life in Year One*, 88.

> He has shown strength with his arm
> He has scattered the proud in their vanity
> He has put down the mighty from their thrones
> And exalted those of low degree.
> He has filled the hungry with good things
> And the rich he has sent empty away.

If we believe that these are, more or less, Mary's words, they are bold words to be spoken in Roman-dominated Judea and Galilee. Is she thinking of the men that took her family's livelihood to make themselves obscenely rich while driving her father into poverty?

Such an economic turn would drive young men out of farming, as only so many tenant farmers would be needed. Mary's oldest brother Jacob will take his father's place working the farm which they tenant; Jeremiah will follow the men that head up the road early most mornings to work in Sepphoris. The construction of the splendid, Roman-style city of Sepphoris, built to glorify Herod and Caesar, would probably draw off the few young men not needed for farming to be *tektons*, which the Gospels translate as "carpenters." But *tektons* would work with everything, from carvings, to stone work as well as wood work. The Christmas cards show Joseph working in a carpentry shop. But it's just as likely to see him setting stones in place up a scaffold in the Roman-style city under construction.

But Joseph is hardly in the picture yet. Mary has seen him around the village, with the other young men and her brother Jeremiah, heading up on foot in the first morning light, carrying large and small hammers, saws, large chisels, and pry bars, the tools of their trade, on their way to construct the glory of Rome and the glory of King Herod in Sepphoris. She thinks him handsome, with his new beard and the long curls dangling from his sideburns in front of his ears. She notices that he watches her back. She remembers five years ago when he stood up in the synagogue and read out a blessing before the reading of the Torah, thus entering his manhood. They have never really spoken. And like all women, she keeps her plain, brown, woolen veil over her head when she goes into the village. (Sorry, no blue. Dye is for rich people, not poor girls like Mary.) It is easy to glance at the handsome young men and then hide your eyes behind your woolen veil. Though Mary is a little alarmed and curious that on two occasions, she has taken a second glance and found Joseph looking at her.

At this point, I can't say whether the Joseph Mary sees is not only older, but already married and widowed, being the father of James, Joses, Jude, and Simon, as well as three daughters, or whether she sees Joseph as an eligible young man in her village.[2] The older widower is the way Catholics and the Orthodox would have it. Protestants prefer to believe that Jacob, Josef, Judah, and Shimon (their real names without Hellenizing them) are yet-to-be-born future sons of Mary herself.

For the purposes of this meditation I'm going to go with the second option. I realize this puts me on the Protestant side of the issue, but I am willing to stand corrected on this matter should better evidence arise. And I really, really, really don't know. Currently, the evidence is all over the place. For every indication towards one conclusion, there is counter-evidence for the opposite conclusion. The first and somewhat telling piece of evidence leans toward Jesus having step-brothers and step-sisters. This is when Mary and Jesus' brothers come to straighten him out in Matthew 12:47 and Luke 8:20. Such behavior would not be quite so possible were Jesus the eldest, son of a dead father and therefore head of household. Such behavior is more in line with James, the eldest, having a serious talk with his little step-brother. Of course, this is nowhere near conclusive. If Joseph has existing family, sons and daughters, and married Mary as a second wife after the death of his first, where were they when Joseph took Mary to Bethlehem and Jesus was born? And where were they when the family fled to Egypt? It's entirely possible that the Protestant view is correct and that Mary had eight children, Jesus being but the first. But that raises other questions. If James were the next-oldest brother, and we know he was around after the crucifixion, because he is mentioned in 1 Corinthians 15, as a leader in the Christian movement at Jerusalem, why does Jesus give his mother, Mary, to John, son of Zebedee, at the cross? And even if James were son of Joseph and a first wife, why wouldn't he step up and take care of his father's second wife? Families did things like that. The rampant individualism which is so American, where we cut ties with all but our nuclear family (and sometimes with them as well) is not known in first-century Palestine. As if this were not enough to stir controversy, the Greek word for cousin is ξαδερφος, or in English spelling, *xaderfos*,. When the word used in Matthew 12:47 and Luke 8:20, it is αδελφός, or *adelphos*, that is, "brother." Catholic and Orthodox writers since the time of St Jerome

---

2 Mark 6:3, Matthew 13:55-56

have been telling us that *adelphos* could just as easily translate as "cousin." But if so, why is there another Greek word for cousin?

The controversy is hopeless. So I will just go with the second option for the sake of this meditation, admitting that I may well be wrong. And sadly the main reason the controversy exists at all is because so many Christians need Mary to be ever-virgin in order to satisfy their unconscious Manichaee and Gnostic tendency to equate celibacy with holiness.

Yet, despite the fact that this issue is loudly controversial, this is not really nearly as important as the other point I was trying to make above. And that is, Mary is like Jesus, because Jesus is like Mary. It's DNA. It's the raising Jesus had. Chances are they looked like fraternal twins but for their ages. Certainly the Lord got all his human DNA from his mother, the Holy Spirit being his father. This leads to a rather tenuous but interesting idea. We have the face from the Shroud of Turin, which has stumped most of the scientific attempts to declare it a fraud, but is, of course, unprovable as true. In it, Christ has a long oval face, deep-set, slightly wide eyes, a long, thin, straight nose, and high cheek bones. The beard obscures his jaw line, though he seems to have a pointed chin. If this is the face of Jesus Christ, it is also, by the DNA which he solely inherits from her, the face of Maryam of Nazareth. She is no Northern-Italian beauty, nor Amish white girl with brown hair, pretty eyes (by the standards of the American make-up industry), round-cheeked girl with a button nose, looking like she was on sedatives.

She had, if this is accurate, a long oval face, deep-set, slightly wide eyes, a long, thin, straight nose, and high cheek bones. Recently, I had a Mexican-American student, a young woman, who exactly fit this description. So, this is why I believe the Mary of Tepeyac Hill probably looked like the real Maryam of Nazareth more than any other appearance.

But this connection on the physical and the personality level between Maryam and her son, I will continue to follow. But for now, since she was seven, Maryam has been the woman of the house. Certainly, after the death of her mother, her aunts and older cousins came in to help, but Maryam has slowly absorbed all the domestic chores, plus any farm-work around the house she can find time to do.

The question comes up here about all those years. Most biographies are full of change and events. Even if I could actually hop into Dr Who's tardis and observe Maryam, I doubt I could produce that. She has had the daily life of a pre-industrial peasant woman, with no interest and no dynamic events. She has never traveled up to this point, farther than a couple

MEDITATION THREE: A BEGINNING

of miles from Nazareth. She has met no famous authors or actors or not been encouraged in her creativity or to seek education. She cooks, she cleans, she washes. She feeds the animals. She sleeps and she does it again. The only break for her is Shabbat, when all work stops and meals are what we'd now call left-overs. She listens to her father read from the Torah and the prophets. She listens to him read the Psalms.

Romanticism and the seeing of divinity in nature is still centuries away, but she likes Psalm 24 about the earth being the handiwork of the God of her people, the God of Abraham, Issac, Jacob, and Moses, known as Yahweh, or sometimes El. Yahweh's name is rarely spoken aloud, being too sacred. Heli and the men refer to him as "*Adonai*", the Lord. Yet, their very names as a family are full of the unspoken name. Her brother, "yirmiya", or Jeremiah in the Greek, means "exalted by Ya(weh)". Her cousin Elisheva's name means "El is my oath." Yahweh is all around them. She feels his presence both in her heart and in the ritual baths they take, the Law they follow, which means she will never taste pork, and he is in their very names that mean who they are, and their common name as a people, Isra-EL." On her few breaks from an endless cycle of work, she walks outside and takes in the beauty of the sky and the fields. It is but a moment, and she has not the freedom to launch into a movie version of the hills being alive with the sound of music. Chores await her. But her heart is moved nevertheless.

She has not been alone; extended families took care of one another, and as we return to that extended family gathering, she is thick with the girl cousins her own age, as likely as not discussing prospective husbands. But Maryam was born around Passover time, in the Spring, and she has passed her thirteenth Passover. No one remembers specific birth dates in a culture with no written calendars and only astronomical or weather events to help them tell the years. She spends her time now with her cousin, Dvorah ("Deborah" in Greek), her aunt, Rachel, who has been sharing the knowledge of herbal healing, and with her much older cousin, Elisheva ("Elizabeth" in the Greek), with whom she is very close. Elisheva was fortunate enough to catch the eye of an older Levite man, Zechariah, and has been married some years now, but without child. A sadness covers Elisheva, but they are all glad to see one another as all the women cousins and aunts cluster together in one place, while the men and boys cluster elsewhere.

And Maryam is the topic of all the whispering and laughter of cousins and aunts. She has had her first bleeding and her first ritual bath that follows menstruation. Ready or not, she's a woman now. And the husband talk flies, cousins and aunts speculating on who would be a good match and laughing at their play. Maryam laughs too and probably feels awkward with all the attention on her. But she also has great empathy, and she feels their joy. She is not very self-conscious about them focusing on her because her mind is on their joy and not her own self-image. How un-21st century. This is another place where Mary is like Jesus because Jesus is like Mary. Christ had a vast empathy. Would his mother have less? And all the appearances she has made across the centuries, almost invariably are about mercy or generosity, or giving in some fashion. She cannot leave us alone because she cannot stop caring. Protestants will say here, "you're talking about Jesus." Yes, him too. But Mary gives it to him and gets it from him in the same motion. Another paradox? God seems to be terribly fond of creating paradoxes. The Creator of the Universe born in a barn; the Son of God rejected from the Temple that worshiped his Father, and in trinitarian terms, himself. It's almost a sign of the Lord's work if something is paradoxical.

Dvorah whispers, "I hear Joseph ben Jacob has been talking about you and asking if your father has chosen you a husband yet. . . . "

Another cousin interrupts, "I heard Joel ben Eliezar asks about you . . . "

More laughter. Maryam believes none of it.

But in spite of the good feeling of being surrounded by women who love her, Maryam is uneasy about the talk of a husband. Not only the uncertainty of this future troubles her, but the thought that she would have to leave an already weak and ill father to other hands to care for. Jacob is eleven now and will be old enough to take a wife in two more seasons. The farm house they rent from the land-lord and the job of tending the fields, will fall to him. Jeremiah is only nine, but time flies swiftly. Three or four more seasons and he too will read before the Torah in the synagogue and be a man. Like many second sons, he will go to the work battalions of *tektons* that go to Sepphoris every day to work on Herod's great city. Father does his best in the fields, but he would have to give up their house to the landlord if not for Jacob's labor in the fields with him. It was an evil day when Lucius bought their land with the soldiers standing behind him. Lucius may be a Jew, but as his Roman name implied, he had left the following of Yahweh behind for Roman ways and was now the wealthiest man in the vicinity. He was not known for his generosity either. Farmers who gave him trouble or grew old and weak were thrown from their homes. Everything depended on Jacob's ability to cover for Heli and then take the lease when Heli could

MEDITATION THREE: A BEGINNING

do no more. The alternative is beggary and starving in the streets. Mary has cause to ponder these things in her heart.

And the land doesn't yield like it should. The old cycle of rotating crops that her father and all the other farmers used to do has been replaced with the same crop year after year, depleting the soil, all because it is the most profitable for Lucius, who owns all these farms. They all know it. They dare not challenge Lucius. The might of Herod and Rome stands behind him. Maryam would like to say something to him anyway, but as a woman, she is not allowed. Here again, as Mary is like Jesus, Jesus is like Mary. Jesus never hesitated to tell truth to power, and it is part of what got him killed. Maryam, whose song celebrates the rich and powerful being cast down, is the same. Jacob and Jeremiah, even Heli, are hesitant to push their daughter and sister. Maryam has been known to administer a quick, abrupt, and brutally accurate retort. We choke at this thought. The Christmas-card, Amish-girl Mary is so serene and sedated. Yes, she is. And it just shows that we perceive feminine perfection as silent and accepting of male dominance. Another mirror instead of a window. This is why we keep our image of Mary sedated. But I have to ask myself, would a sedate woman, embracing her gender inferiority, write something as bold and combative as the Magnificat? I don't think so.

There are young men who under their breath mutter about rising up against Rome and driving them out like the Maccabees. Maryam feels their anger, though she doubts that it would lead to much more than the destruction of Israel. Yahweh must come down and save them again. But what would be the point of that if they are like Lucius? The ones like Herod and Lucius always end up ruling, even the Maccabees, turning from liberators to tyrants to Sadducees. Maryam remembers what her father has told her of the history of her people. Even Solomon was seduced by his prosperity and his foreign wives and their gods. No, if Yahweh came again and saved his people, he would first have to save them from their own hearts, and their pursuit of the gods of prosperity and power. He would have to write his Law on all their hearts, or it would merely be a bloody repetition of the Maccabee revolt, which granted independence just long enough for the Maccabees to become proud tyrants, and for the Romans to replace the Greeks as their oppressors. Only Yahweh changing all their hearts would bring the kingdom, and dare she even think it, the Messiah. This is much for a poor, country-girl to be contemplating, but amongst Maryam's people, though few could read and all those who could were men, by their customs they were people of the Book and their memories were long.

The day after the family feast, Maryam is contemplating these things as she carries the large, clay water pot to the well for the second time in a day. So she was startled when a man's voice addressed her.

"Good day, Maryam."

Maryam turns so fast, so startled, that her woolen veil falls and her long, black hair is uncovered. She puts down her jar to cover up again; it is the respectable thing to do. "Good day, Joseph ben Jacob," she replies.

"I did not mean to startle you," he apologizes.

She dares to look up and see that he has lowered his eyes. There is no pushy, aggressive air around him. He is as modest a man, she realizes, as she tries to be as a woman. She appreciates this. She even smiles at him. He looks up and smiles back. He is an older man, she thinks, already eighteen and not yet married. The gossip in the town is that Joseph ben Jacob will never marry. He seems tongue-tied, now that he has her attention. She realizes he's trying to make conversation, but that he is bound by some sort of feeling—for her. Her empathy senses this quickly.

She helps him out. "Why are you not bound for Sepphoris today?"

He sighs, and she knows that he is relieved to be back on familiar ground. "They ran out of stone for two days, so they have laid us off. Maryam, I wanted to . . . I mean I would like to ask . . . Oh! Let me fill your water jug!" Sudden action seems to relieve him from the burden of the thing that he wants to ask. She sees he's sweating and it is a hot day in Palestine, but not so hot as that. As he's bringing up the bucket from the well, and moves the full bucket toward her jar, she realizes that he is proposing. That explains why she so often caught him looking at her as the men walked out of town on the road. That explains why Dvorah at the family gathering was so sure of rumors that he wanted to marry her. Dvorah had heard correctly.

Long courtships were not done and women not allowed to "date" young men till they knew. Men selected a bride with their parents' concurrence and then made an offer family to family. Marriage was a family affair. Romance of the type expected in our time was unknown. But a girl, if she were lucky, might speak to the young man first, if he respected her wishes enough.

Joseph was not required to seek Maryam's willingness first. He could have assured success by going straight to her father, who would have approved of course, Joseph being a young man of honor, and then Maryam would have had no choice. But instead he chose to wait for her to come alone to the well, risking the chance that she would say no, not forcing his will on her. Her heart warmed. It was an extremely respectful thing to do, making himself vulnerable to her will, and Maryam admires him more now for doing the hard thing of talking to her first before going to her father. He respected her enough to give her a choice. Not many men respected women so.

Joseph wrestles the heavy water bucket to ground level and pours it efficiently into Maryam's water jar. Maryam senses not only his strength, which is considerable—he heaves the heavy water-laden bucket around like a toy—but his kindness and his own empathy, in thinking of what she might need and how he might help her even without being asked.

Maryam decides to help him. "Joseph ben Jacob, you wanted to ask me something."

He stands up tall, a strong young man. "I wanted to ask . . . . I wanted to ask . . . ."

Maryam decides. This seems odd to us now, but she has little choice, and this is a better choice than many she might be forced to make later. To find a kind and honest man who might ask her hand was all a young woman could hope for. Falling in love was still centuries away. "Yes," she says.

"Yes? But I haven't said, . . . I mean, if you might consider being my wife . . ."

"I said yes."

His eyes get big and his mouth falls slightly open. "Yes?"

"Yes, I will marry you, Joseph ben Jacob, if my father consents."

"Oh, this is wonderful. I will talk to your father . . . "

"Come to our house and eat the evening meal with us, after the sun goes down and my father comes in from the fields. You may talk to him then. Bring your father as well."

"I will," he says, barely containing his obvious joy. He runs off like a boy. She laughs softly and hoists up her jar, heading for home. Well, she went out to get water and came back with a betrothal. How's that for a day's work?

She comes around the corner past several houses, until her own house appears around the bend and a thought comes to her: women don't stand in synagogue and read before the Torah reading to establish their womanhood. But for good or ill, whatever fate Yahweh might send, she was now a woman. Childhood was completely over in this, her thirteenth year. She sighs, and resumes walking. Dinner wasn't going to prepare itself.

Meditation Four: Whenever It Rains, It Pours

I HAVE NOTICED THAT life seems to go for long stretches of repetition and "the usual", punctuated with startling changes, not always pleasant. If you feel I haven't narrated enough of Maryam's childhood, I reply, she didn't have one. At least she did not have a childhood in the sense that we, post-Romantics that we are, think of a childhood. Or if she did, it would be similar to the childhood of some Bedouin girl today. There would be little time for play; working for basic survival took all one's time and energy. Then before you know it, you're grown and the burden is on your shoulders. There were no piano lessons, no ballet class, no schooling of any kind other than to listen to father read from the Torah and the Writings.

Now I want you to hold that thought and then go back to something I've already said: out of billions of women to be born to humanity, God picked *this one*. Why didn't he pick some highly refined Chinese or European princess? Why didn't he pick a Sumerian or an Egyptian, or a Greek or Roman from some high civilization? Or perhaps an Aztec, or an Inca, or a Mayan girl? Well, part of the answer was that the Messiah would come from Israel, which narrows the field. But notice the timing. This is not an Israel proudly independent which could give a girl a rich raising from the depth of its civilization. This is an Israel conquered and impoverished, that has long lost its independence, handed off from Assyrian to Babylonian, to Egyptian, to Greek, to Roman overlords like worn goods. I'm not necessarily disparaging civilization or education for women. I believe in education for all children. But the quality that God values, that he has instilled in this girl is not anything that can be taught or given in childhood. That is why I think that her gift, whatever it was, call it immaculate conception or ever-virginity if you need to, was a grace. It was something given her which she did not earn. In a sense, she was not better than any other woman ever born, except that he made her better. If that meets your definition of immaculate conception, well fine. And I suppose some of us who still confuse flesh with evil need to think that this thing can be reduced to endless virginity. If that's the best you can do to grasp it, I suppose it will have to do. My problem with that point of view is mainly is that the Buddha Mary, floating painlessly and perfect above human existence in an untouchable force-field of eternal virginity—that Mary is not a human being. That is a myth that says more about our need to imagine that the spiritual is beyond our reach, and therefore we don't need to try for holiness ourselves. It's about that and has nothing to do with any reality involving Maryam of Nazareth, wife of Joseph ben Jacob.

But let us again, like Scrooge and the Ghost of Christmas Present, step invisibly into the central courtyard of Heli's farmhouse. Maryam has been baking bread for hours now and has acquired some salted, dried fish shipped over from Capernaum. They were expensive, and she sacrificed two precious coins for them, but this was an important dinner. In case anyone is confused about names, surnames or "last names" as we know them, they don't arrive until the Middle Ages. Common names like Jacob and Joseph were often repeated. The way to distinguish one from another was to name the father as well. "Ben" here is Hebrew for "son of." Thus Maryam's fiancé is Joseph ben Jacob and her brother is Jacob ben Heli. But let us go back to Maryam in the kitchen, setting up everything to feed not only her father and brothers, but two more mouths as well.

She also makes a trip out to the fields and tells her father that Joseph ben Jacob and his father, Jacob ben Matthan were coming to the evening meal, and to ask her brother Jacob to finish up there so that father could come in to clean up a bit for his guests. Inviting guests such as these is not too common a practice in a poor household and her father guesses easily as to what's up.

Walking back from the field together, Heli asks, "So Joseph has made you an offer?"

"Yes, Papa."

"What have you said to him?"

"I said I was willing if you approved."

"You know I like Joseph ben Jacob. Of course I approve. Will you be happy with such a husband?"

"He is a good man, Papa, and kind."

"Yes, that is the necessary thing." Heli puts his arm around her. "If it pleases you, I am glad, for I could not have said no to such a man. But I am glad that your heart is in this choice."

"But Papa, when I marry, who will cook for you?" She really means who will take care of him, but she doesn't want to hurt his pride by telling him that she has noticed his increasing ill health and weakness. And not two months ago, he lay in bed for some minutes on a morning, half-conscious and unable to move his left arm and leg. His eyes did not focus and he muttered to her from the right side of his mouth only. Maryam prayed, kneeling at his side, her face wet with tears, and then he startled her. He woke and rose easily, as if nothing had been wrong, not remembering anything about it. The boys had been gone. Only she had witnessed it. But Maryam feared for her father's life.

"We will manage, my girl."

Maryam is not so sure.

The meal is jolly, with Heli laughing and talking with Jacob ben Matthan. Of course they have known each other since boyhood. Joseph makes a formal request for Maryam's hand and Heli consents, blessing the couple. A *Kettubah* contract, brought by Jacob ben Matthan, is signed by him and Heli. The betrothal is officially sealed. When the guests have left and Maryam has cleaned up the cooking area, Heli goes to his room off the courtyard where he sleeps. Jacob and Jeremiah go to their sleeping room, and Maryam goes to hers. Her window is high up, but she positions her sleeping pallet so that as she is lying there, drifting to sleep, she sees the stars wheeling above in Yahweh's Heaven.

And then life goes on. Joseph will need a month or two of work at Sepphoris to raise the bride price and then a wedding feast can be set. Easy. This sort of thing happened nearly every day somewhere in first-century Israel. And if we were standing there with the Ghost of Christmas Present and didn't know any better, we'd all have taken bets that this young woman was bound to become just another housewife and mother in conquered Israel. But then the miracle happens, striking silently, a beam of light in the darkness.

And this pattern is actually the rule and not the exception. Even in Jesus' very public miracles, like the feeding of the thousands, the whole thing came as a complete surprise to everyone concerned. We tend to think of large and public miracles like the parting of the Red Sea and think that that is Yahweh's MO. But those sort of miracles are rare. God is far more likely to surprise us, and do it in such a way that no matter how hard we try, we can't prove our miracle to anyone else. Even when Maryam's Son raised Jairus' sick little daughter, he allowed almost no one in the room with her but himself.

Moses saw many large and public miracles, but for him it all started with a burning bush that only he witnessed. In a very real sense, the miraculous with Israel's God tends to be personal and private.

So Maryam lays down to sleep on another such night, after a day's mundane work in her father's house, on the mundane straw pallet, in her mundane sleeping room, decorated only by the stars coming through the window. It is the month of *Tammuz*, and summer with its oppressive heat, is coming. And then suddenly, without any warning, a blazing light explodes from the corner by the door and a large figure looms like a lava fissure, looking more like a column of incandescence than anything human. A weird voice comes from the light. Maryam sits up, startled and amazed, putting an arm up over her eyes as this strange thing blinds her with its brilliance. May Yahweh protect her, she prays.

"Hail, favored of Yahweh, who is with you!" the voice from the blinding light echoes in unearthly tones.

Maryam's heart is pounding and she thinks she will soon die.

The voice continues, "Do not be afraid, Maryam, for you have found favor with Yahweh. You will conceive a son, and you will name him Jeshua. He will be great and be called the Son of the Most High. And *Adonai* will give to him the throne of his father, David, and he will reign over the house of Jacob forever, and of his Kingdom there will be no end."

Now this is the part of the story that so many people miss, even if they've heard it a thousand times. Part of the problem with the Gassy Marys and the Amish-girl Marys is that they are calm, meek, and obedient women. And I think for many of us, we imagine Mary at this point says, "Yes Lord" with her hands palms-together and her eyes lowered in female modesty, in her Super-Virginal Buddha posture.

That is utter nonsense.

Any sort of woman who had so little will as that, as to be a "yes-woman" to all male commands, would have very little spine, by definition. She would scream at seeing Gabriel and start trying to climb out the window. Or she might just faint dead away. If you, as a human being, have spent your whole life throwing your will and your self-direction away to the opposite gender, you are going to be confused when confronted with a such a choice in a dramatically startling form. Such a Mary, if she had any presence of mind, would excuse herself and ask to bring her father into the conversation so that he could decide for her. Throw the "feminist" word at me if you want, but I just cannot see how a spineless Mary would have done much more than babble incoherently at the sight of an archangel.

What does she do?

Luke's text says that she was troubled and tried to discern what sort of visit this might be.[1] Hardly surprising, and the detail here is only something Maryam would have known, which makes me think again that Luke interviewed her at length before writing his gospel. We hear this part of the story every Christmas and the obvious thing about it just passes us by. Maryam of Nazareth had a cool head. As a retired teacher I've known two types in the teachers I've worked with. Some panic at the first sight of trouble, raging and running around. Others, no disaster could possibly faze them, but that they immediately begin to deal quietly and effectively with the crisis, keeping their cool head. Maryam here has a cool head. She is working this out in her mind. She's no dumb female. Her mind races to the two most important things to get out of this surprising visit: 1) boy, this is going to cause a problem, ("was troubled") and 2) just what is in the fine print here? ("and tried to discern") She speaks number 3, which is 'just how do I get pregnant all by myself?' I don't know what an archangel might have anticipated, but he gets a cool cross-examination questioning worthy of a veteran district attorney. In another life, Maryam of Nazareth might have made a good lawyer.

She says, "How will this be, since I am a virgin?"

She may live in a primitive pre-industrial world, but she knows enough biology to know that men make women pregnant. Some people act as if everyone in the pre-industrial world was stupid, just because they didn't have access to our level of scientific knowledge.

Gabriel replies in detail to his cross-examiner, "The Holy Spirit will come upon you, and the power of the Most High will overshadow you; therefore the child to be born will be called holy—the Son of God. And mark my words, your relative Elisheva in her old age has also conceived a son, and this is the sixth month with her who was barren. For nothing will be impossible with God."

One thing that Catholic teaching makes very clear here, and I believe they are absolutely right, is that this is a choice. Maryam could have said, "No! Not me!" And the Catholic teaching is that God would have respected that refusal. I would agree with that. The God that respects human free will

---

1. Luke 1:29

to the point that he lets us pollute our world with our own evil, that God isn't going to force the hand of a farmer's daughter.

For Maryam, the next few moments must have felt like they lasted a million years. Gabriel has handed her not only the full picture, but a way of verifying in checking up on cousin Elisheva, and the final thesis statement, the whole point to the whole message: Nothing, nothing is impossible with God. What she says next proves how much spine, how much *chutzpah* she had, this tough-minded, sharp, thirteen-year-old girl. For she knew instantly that everyone she loved would turn against her, her brothers, her father, her fiancé, and that this might get her stoned to death. The archangel was not promising an easy ride, rather the opposite. Things were just about to get very real in multiple unpleasant ways. But at the same time, all that she'd been thinking about a Messiah to turn around the hearts, and maybe even the fate of her poor, enslaved country, rose up in her heart. She was to be the vehicle for this thing to come to pass. Her son, *her* son was to be the deliverer. She might go down in flames, but her son would conquer.

She pulls her scraps of courage together and says, "Look, I am Yahweh's servant. Let it happen to me as you have said."

The world shook.

But as often happens when something miraculous occurs, the following day comes like a Monday after a weekend in our culture. Something spectacular happens, and it is immediately followed by the troublesome and the mundane.

Does she tell her father?

Does she tell Joseph?

But as I said earlier, though Maryam was beset with doubts as much as any of us would be, I believe she "set her face" toward this thing. Even if everything went wrong and she died, she would follow the path Yahweh had set in front of her in such a dramatic fashion. There are times when trust takes the form of saying to yourself, "Whatever happens, I'm going to follow this through and take the consequences."

So resigning herself to take the worst, the following day Maryam finds Joseph in the market and takes him aside, telling him plainly about the archangel and all that happened to her, and that she is pregnant.

He says nothing, but the wounded look in his eyes tells her plainly that he doesn't believe her and thinks she has betrayed him. He walks away without speaking.

Maryam's heart stings, but she has set her face. This disaster belongs to Yahweh, and it's up to him what happens next.

The day passes and her father is in the fields. She may have determined her course, but she is not up to facing down both Joseph and Heli in one day. So when her father and the boys come in for the evening meal she suggests something.

"Papa, Aunt Rachel, Dvorah, and my uncles are going to Judea this week to sacrifice at the temple for our newborn cousin. They will be gone three months. Could I travel with them? I wish to see Elisheva, for I am told she is with child. I can help her in her pregnancy."

"Maryam, you have worked so hard for all of us. I can spare you for some months."

So, without a goodbye to Joseph, she has a small satchel and her walking stick and is wearing her best and sturdiest sandals the following morning. She is standing in the market place with Dvorah talking softly. They are waiting for their uncles to pull the train of travelers together. Twice now Dvorah has asked what is wrong, and Maryam has declined to answer. She is thinking to herself that the trip will be sad.

Without warning she feels a gentle hand on her shoulder. She turns around and it is Joseph. Kindness is in his eyes.

"I heard you were going to Judea."

"For three months, Joseph. I will see my kin and return. I did not think you would miss me."

"Can we talk?" He looks at Dvorah, who excuses herself and walks away.

"Joseph," Maryam begins, "I did not mean to hurt you, but . . . ."

"No," he interrupts. "I was . . . visited . . . in a dream last night. *Adonai* spoke and told me. I know you are speaking the truth now. But it is difficult to understand."

Maryam squeezes his hand in happiness and relief. "I'm not sure I understand it either. People will think we were impatient. Papa will scold us, but he will forgive."

"Let them think what they will," Joseph answers. "It is what *Adonai* wants that is the important thing."

"Yes," she agrees.

"I look forward to your return," he says.

And so Maryam makes the days of the journey in much more peace of heart. Three days later she walks into the home of Zechariah and

Elisheva, after a long and dusty, and yes, mundane trip skirting Samaria and into Judea.

For as she enters the room of Elisheva's house, calling Elisheva, her cousin astonishes her, blurting out, "Blessed are you among all of us women, and blessed is the fruit of your womb! And why is it granted to me that the mother of my Lord should come to me? Believe me, when I heard your voice calling me, the baby in my womb leapt for joy. And blessed is she who believed that there would be a fulfillment of what was spoken to her by *Adonai*."

Scripture tells us that Maryam broke into the canticle we now call the Magnificat. And I do believe it came from her. But being a poet myself, I find that first inspirations often undergo much editing. But I still believe she created the essential piece because it's not what a patriarchal society would put in the mouth of a woman.

Her soul magnifies the Lord. The Greek verb is Μεγαλύνει. *Megalynei* would be the English spelling. And it means to magnify. There is no translation mistake here. This is an interesting choice of verbs, assuming that God is something that we could in our weak human natures, magnify. But it's not God that needs magnifying here, but our own limited, human perception of him that does. Maryam recognizes immediately that it's humanity that needs to wake up and realize God's power. And her intent is to be part of the slap that awakens them. The poem, or perhaps song, goes on.

> For he has looked on the humbleness of his servant
> And see, from now on all generations will call me blessed
> For he, the mighty does greatness for me.
> And holy is his name.
> And his mercy is for those who fear him
> From generation to generation.
> Scattering the proud in the thoughts of their hearts
> Brought down the mighty from thrones
> Exalted the humble
> Filled the hungry with good things
> And the rich sent empty
> Helped his servant Israel
> Remembering mercy
> As he spoke to our fathers,
> Abraham and his offspring forever.

I've cut out some of the intervening words translators add here and put in only the English equivalents of mainly the actual Greek words. This will make it not read easily, but I want the reader to see what parts of it are Maryam's. It really reads like a laundry list for social revolution.

What's remarkable beyond the fierce tone of this song, from a woman in a patriarchal society, is its political and historical awareness. Though I don't have the reference, I can almost wager that some scholar has decided that later writers put these words in Maryam's mouth for this passage. I don't believe that. Put it down to what I call "women-in-camp-phenomenon," but I think this Jewish girl came up with the basic version, in spite of minor editing later. It would make her rather determined, rather assertive, rather bold, politically astute. And I believe that she had these qualities because her son did.

One does not simply piss off Maryam of Nazareth and walk away unscathed.

One thing it does tell me about her is that she has not missed the bitter lessons of the injustice of Herod's economic policies and cronyism in Galilean politics. And it tells me that she expects this son in her womb, that came to her in a vastly unusual way, to deliver a counter-attack. Maryam is militant, to put it simply. But militant feelings ran very high in Israel in those days. They finally boiled over after the death and Resurrection of her son, and turned into a bloody and futile revolution that sent the surviving Jews into exile.

I want to take some time here to address the growing tension in my account between what a woman can and can't do in the ancient world. I don't want to be feminist in the sense, that like Hazleton, I project my own ideas, and thus make this another foggy mirror. I referred above to the "women-in-camp-phenomenon". Let me explain this, and what it has to do with Maryam of Nazareth. When I was an undergraduate, I minored in Native American Studies. At one point I undertook a thorough and multi-year research project into the pre-reservation *Tsistsistas* people, known to Americans as the Cheyenne. These were mounted hunter-gatherers, plains Indians, who lived, at least superficially, in a patriarchal society. But one older man confessed in an interview about pre-reservation life, that though the men ruled in war and in hunting, activities outside the camp, nothing went on inside the camp without the women's consent. This is what I call "women-in-camp-phenomenon." Patriarchy may rule on the surface, but most women in history, and across cultures, find ways to circumvent the theory.

It's not just in pre-industrial Native Americans that we see this. Chaucer's *Canterbury Tales* gives us Allison, the Wife of Bath. Allison lives in patriarchal 15th century England, where she defies all the rules as to what women can do, whether or not they can own a business, and whether or not they can be independent of a man in the community. Chaucer makes fun of Allison's husbands' futile attempts to tame her, and one senses that he has little respect for the idea that men rule. Chaucer must have gotten his model from somewhere. We might see Allison as a "loose woman" and perhaps some would attempt to scold her for being too free with her tongue. But Allison defeats patriarchy in the 1400s and I have a hard time believing she was the only one. I suspect that women like her were rather common, and Chaucer is enjoying that fact in the humorous way in which he is pointing this out. Chaucer himself does not seem offended by her. The tone of his descriptions makes it apparent that he finds her interesting, amusing, and perhaps he even admires her.

Thus when I look at Maryam, yes, she toes the official line for what a woman can and cannot do. She marries with her father's permission, and takes Joseph as a better choice, because she is aware that her father can and will at some point force her to marry his choice. Better to manipulate the system and choose Joseph while her father is minded to agree with her. And her remark to Joseph about not missing her is in part a way of getting her fiancé's permission to leave town. Maryam knows her life will be ruled by men for the foreseeable future. The feminist revolution is still twenty centuries away, and Maryam isn't trying to start it here and now.

At the same time, I believe that history is filled with many "Wives of Bath." Not all are as saucy and sexually manipulative as Chaucer's Allison, but I thoroughly believe that women have been gaming the system whenever they have been confronted with patriarchy for thousands of years. That's not to say it always worked, and men can be brutal and violent. But an exploration of world literature will find many instances of women stepping out of assigned roles. Think of *Mu Lan* in China, that Disney made into a film. Think of the examples amongst the people of Israel, the prophetess Dvorah (Deborah), or Judith, who de-capitated Holofernes, or Esther, celebrated in Purim, who risked her life to save the Jews from a vast pogrom in Persia.

Even amongst the *Tsistsistas* people, there is an account at the Battle of the Rosebud, a few days before the Little Bighorn, when a *Tsistsistas* warrior was shot out of the saddle. His sister, named Buffalo Calf Road Woman, jumped on a horse and without getting hit, rode to her fallen brother, got his inert body up on the horse and rode back into Sioux and Cheyenne lines. The *Tsistsistas* call the battle "The Fight where the Girl Saved her Brother." The warriors were so impressed with her, that she rode to battle again a few days later against Custer. To this day, she is honored in Cheyenne history.

You can impose the patriarchal system on women; they will find ways to go around it. They always have. Nothing happens in camp without the women's consent.

So I see this determined, smart, young woman, Maryam of Nazareth, both paying homage to the system that tells her that her father and husband will rule her, but finding ways to do what she knows is right and is determined to do. She has "set her face."

Look out, world.

Meditation Five: One Wild Christmas

As I said before, weekends turn into Mondays, and spectacular welcomings like Elizabeth (Elisheva) gave Maryam stay in the memories. But we know Maryam stayed three months, probably to assist Elisheva's pregnancy and keep the household running when morning sickness or some other side effect of pregnancy makes doing their routine chores impossible. And many pregnancies are particularly difficult. The three-month length of Maryam's stay makes me think that Elisheva's was not an easy one. Maryam probably stayed through the birth of her young cousin, Johanan, known to us as St John the Baptist. In any case, the greeting at arrival and the assisting of the midwives to deliver Zechariah's son, and to witness the surprising return of his ability to speak, were high points. Changing soiled bedding and mopping up vomit, and emptying chamber pots, as well as doing someone else's cooking and cleaning for three months was the lion's share of the visit. But isn't this always the way of things when we are called by God to a way of life? There may be a mountaintop experience to confirm our calling. But most of what we have to do is slogging. I doubt it was any different for Maryam.

By the time her donkey stops at the marketplace in Nazareth, Joseph is waiting for her. She has the beginnings of a baby bump and there's no hiding the fact now. People talk behind their hands at Maryam and Joseph and she can easily guess what they're saying. "Boy, those two crazy kids. Couldn't even wait for the wedding feast before consummating the marriage." Like Joseph, Maryam decides to just let tongues wag and ignore it.

Explaining to Heli goes better than Mary had thought. They do not attempt to tell him about angels and dreams and let him think them impetuous. He scolds for but a minute, but the prospect of a grandchild so pleases him, that he soon leaves off. Actually, he is more worried about a marriage feast, which he is supposed to put on. Joseph assures him that he has had much work in Sepphoris the last three months and will cover much of the cost. In the end, in such a small and poor town, with 400 inhabitants with little more than half of that being Jews, the whole Jewish population will come anyway. And many, out of consideration, will contribute food. This reminds me of a line in the first *Lord of the Rings* movie, about Bilbo Baggins' birthday party: half the Shire is invited, and the other half is coming anyway. I suspect any wedding feast in Nazareth was much the same.

The wedding feast soon takes place, minus the wait outside the *chuppah* room, for it is assumed Maryam and Joseph are already lovers. Her baby bump is evidence for that. And the most unforced reading of Matthew 1:25 confirms that Joseph waited till the birth of Jesus before consummating the marriage, something vital in the Jewish mind, despite long and intricate reinterpretations of the passage in defense of ever-virginity. My Catholic and Orthodox sisters and brothers will be scandalized by this, but try thinking here not like a Byzantine or a European, to whom holy goddesses are often virgins, but like a Jew.

According to the website, *Marriage in the Bible and Ancient Marriage and Jewish Wedding Customs,* first-century Jewish marriages/weddings went as follows:

There were three states of a marriage in the Bible:

a. Stage 1: signing the *"ketubbah"* contract (Creating the marriage bond)
   i. The bride would chose her husband and her father would sign a legal contract with him called a *"ketubbah"*.
   ii. Once this is signed the couple is 100% married but do not have sex yet.
   iii. Young children were often married, (arranged marriage) but did not consummate until of age.

b. Stage 2: The *"chuppah"*: sexual consummation.
   i. Up to 7 years later, the groom is able to raise the money as set out in the *ketubbah* contract and notifies the father of the bride, who then sets a date to consummate the marriage at the bride's home.
   ii. The bride waits with her maidens, for the arrival of the groom and his companions.
   iii. The couple enters the *chuppah* room and consummates the marriage while the companions of the bride and groom wait and celebrate outside or in the next room.

    iv. The groom hands the bloodied "proof of virginity cloth" to the witnesses chosen by the bride's parents, who then give it to the bride for safekeeping.
  c. Stage 3: The wedding feast
    i. After consummation, the entire wedding party walks to the house of the groom in a procession for a wedding feast.
    ii. At the conclusion of the wedding feast, the couple has completed the ancient ritual of marriage.

Furthermore, I have seen the same information in other places. Like many pre-industrial societies, the Jews believed that *no marriage took place without sexual consummation*. Our particular brand of spirituality may demand an ever-virgin Mary. But the simple Jewish woman of the first century would have found the idea of celibacy within marriage preposterous, and unthinkable. Notice that it is so important to the Jewish marriage, that the groom has to take his wife's virginity, with everyone standing outside waiting. Then he has to mop up some of the blood from his wife's punctured hymen, and present the cloth to the wedding guests to confirm sexual intercourse took place. They can't just take his word for it—that's how important it is. To put it briefly, in the Jewish mind:

marriage=sex

And as funny as this sounds (which tells me how much we impose our ideas on the past), Mary is not a Catholic girl.

She is a Jew.

We keep mentally slipping off this point with our art portraying Gassy Marys and Amish-girl Marys. Mary and Joseph were Jews. Had they lived in 1930s Germany, they might have gone to Auschwitz. Some people, in their irrational anti-semitism, have even tried to argue that Jesus and his mother were not really Jews. That tells me more about the irrational hatred that consumes them than anything accurate about history.

And we are told in several places in the gospels that Joseph was Maryam's husband. In the Jewish mind that necessarily means that they were lovers. Otherwise they were not married. You can try to work around this all you want but you are just straining the interpretation to do so. But I have labored this point enough.

Before I leave the *chuppah* entirely behind, notice that when Maryam's son tells the parable of the Wise and Foolish Young Women, that the bridegroom they await, symbolizing Christ himself, is arriving to consummate the marriage in the *chuppah* room. For those who think Our Lord was somehow above talking about sex, because their Gnostic tendencies make them think sex is evil, this fact alone indicates that Jesus Christ was not puritanical in mentioning normal and legitimate sex, such as the consummation of a marriage. If this fact makes you wince, you need to check your Gnostic warning device.

Let us return with the Ghost of Christmas Present to silently and invisibly observe the life of Maryam, wife of Joseph. The wedding feast is jolly, for the community uses such events to meet and celebrate and put a little joy in an otherwise poor and overworked existence. People drink wine and talk and laugh. There is dancing, though I suspect it would look more like the dancing at the wedding in *Fidler on a Roof* than what we would do today. Probably men with men and women with women. Joseph dances but Maryam declines, given her state. I like to think that they ran out of wine and that Maryam was embarrassed by that fact. It would explain her being assertive with her son thirty years later at another wedding feast in Cana.

When the feast is over, there is, of course, no honeymoon. Those are still centuries away and for the wealthy. Joseph has no house yet and Maryam's concern for her father's health has led to the couple living in Maryam's room of Heli's house. So as their life settles back into the daily routine, Joseph rises early and joins the men walking the three miles to Sepphoris every morning but Shabbat. He just emerges into the street each morning from a different door than before. At Heli's request, he takes Jeremiah with him, as an apprentice. Maryam's life has changed little except for her growing belly, and the warm man in her bed at night. As she cooks breakfast and makes a mental list of the day's cleaning to be done, she is looking forward to having her baby in her father's house, in the room where the angel appeared, but God seems to love to frustrate our plans. I suspect it's one of the ways he makes us realize the reality of our total dependence on him.

As the months pass and Maryam grows round in the belly, life seems uneventful. Sometimes she wonders about the contrast between her daily existence and the blinding light of the archangel that spoke to her. 21st century people would have doubted their perception. First century people had yet to be stuffed with post-Enlightenment Rationalism. Maryam wonders, but does not doubt. Just when everything seems to be proceeding along like a donkey plodding half-asleep down a dusty road, news comes.

Roman soldiers in their shining steel armor and plumed helmets, march in to the central street of Nazareth from Sepphoris, always a nervous thing. They nail a sign to a post and leave without seeming to notice anyone, obviously feeling superior to the peasants thereabouts. As soon as the soldiers are gone, a crowd gathers around the notice, and Jacob, Maryam's brother is among them.

That night, at the family dinner, Jacob tells the news. By order of the Imperial government, there is to be a census.

"Census," Heli moans. "Census means more taxes."

"There was much grumbling in the market," Jacob observes, tearing his bread and taking a bite. But they all know that no one dares do anything to bring the unwanted attention of Roman soldiers, nor King Herod's guards.

Finally, after a long silence, Joseph says to Heli, "My father, we must go to Bethlehem. It is my family's home."

Heli sighs and waves his hands in the air with futility "And my people also. But I could not make the journey. You will have to go for us. But daughter, you take this journey at such a time. You are so pregnant that you can barely walk straight."

"*Adonai* will see to it," Maryam assures him. She remembers the angel. She remembers thinking she had lost Joseph. She remembers. Yahweh is behind all of this. Things will work out, and usually in surprising ways. That's how Yahweh operated. Maryam knows this.

The walking is too much for her. Joseph would have almost certainly bought or borrowed a donkey for her journey. That part of Christmas art is accurate. There is the long and tedious trek around Samaria, at least three days, past teeming Jerusalem and on to Bethlehem. The town overflows and Joseph is lucky to get a barn for his wife. I always find this interesting because being of the line of David, he would have had relatives in town. But perhaps they too were overwhelmed with other cousins from Galilee and other far points, forced to show up in Bethlehem. It seems to me that the barn they stayed in most likely belonged to a cousin or an uncle. So Joseph's great-uncle Levi, having a house full of visitors and more relations at the crammed inn, offers the young couple the barn. He is apologetic; it's the best he can do. Joseph and Maryam are hoping they can meet the Roman demands and return to Nazareth before Maryam's time comes. God has other plans.

Sitting in the dark in the barn with but one oil lamp, Maryam's water breaks. Shortly after, the first contraction rolls over her like a boulder. She screams in pain. Joseph runs to the house to find the aunts and midwives. The pains are intense and the hours pass. If she was lucky, it was maybe eighteen hours. It may have been twice that. The women of the family take over and tell Joseph to stand back. Aunts Rebekah and Sara, and Joanna, all elder women of long experience, form a circle around Maryam as the pain causes her to cry out loudly.

Our Christmas cards show Joseph and Mary with only animals for company and Mary with the infant in her arms, clean and bundled neatly. It would be a strange Christmas card to show more accurately Joseph standing in the background, helpless, wringing his hands, while a ring of three older women helped a screaming Maryam thrust out her infant son into the world, complete with blood and amniotic fluid.

The Gnostic version has Mary teleport her son painlessly and cleanly out of her womb.

Nonsense.

If Mary's son had to experience the pain of the world, and he is the sinless Son of God, why should she be spared what he was not in terms of pain, dirt, blood, and sweat? But much of the point of the Incarnation in Christianity is that God came down and experienced first-hand the mud, blood, pain, and toil that humans all go through. That's the whole point of the thing, and the incredible testimony to the unfathomable humility of God. Why should Mary be miraculously spared this?

Still, in God's economy, great pain and great joy often go hand-in-hand, though we wish for only the latter. One thing the Christmas cards get right is the picture of Maryam holding her newborn son, Jesus, with wonder and unmitigated love in her eyes. The moment of bonding between mother and child right after birth is profound. And I believe mothers feel attachment and ocean-deep affection for their child to the heights that no man ever really understands. But for Maryam of Nazareth, not only does she adore her son, but playing in the back of her mind is the knowledge that this boy is far more than just another Jewish boy born. She opens her robe and nurses the Son of God for his first meal on Earth.

The hours of childbirth become quiet as Maryam holds her infant son and adores him, as he roots for her nipple. Joseph and the aunts stand around, they having done with the clean up and making ready to take away the mess and afterbirth. As the night draws toward day, the moment is strangely punctuated by local shepherds coming into the barn to worship the child, having seen a fantastic angelic performance in the sky. They tell in detail what they saw, amazing Maryam, Joseph and the three aunts. The child, having nursed, and well-wrapped in swaddling clothes, is laid sleeping in a make-shift crib which is really an animal feeding-trough, known to us as a manger. Again, for Maryam, and now for Joseph, the normal and the mundane, in this case, painful childbirth, is unexpectedly offset by the miraculous. Thus were their lives to be.

In the coming days, Joseph goes into town to report his family and his extended family as well. He stands in line for hours, but the census is over in minutes—Joseph and hundreds others are herded through the main square like cattle to spend thirty seconds answering questions from a Roman scribe at a table. Joseph hopes that they can soon depart for home. But Joseph now has an infant son, and Maryam is nursing. Great-Uncle's Levi's house clears of guests. Joseph and Maryam and Jeshua ben Joseph, known to us and Jesus Christ, are invited to stay in a room in the house as the press and overcrowding vanishes.

After eight days they take the infant to Bethlehem's synagogue and circumcise him, naming him Jeshua, or Jesus in the Greek.

At this point they are visited by Persian astrologers, strange old men in colorful robes, speaking Aramaic in an odd accent, who leave gifts that can be sold for traveling cash. There are arguments over whether Christ was born in December or at another time. The best study I have seen which explains the star and the time of birth is Michael R. Molnar's *The Star of Bethlehem: The Legacy of the Magi*. If Molnar is right, the star was a planetary conjunction that by the astrology of the time could only be interpreted as the birth of a king of the Jews. Molnar has quite of bit of evidence in that much of the Greek pertaining to the star's movements, in Matthew's Gospel is taken straight from the astrological terminology of the time. The astrologers would have found Maryam and Joseph's son by knowing the exact date of the child's birth and asking around Bethlehem for a child born on that day, having been sent to the town by Herod. Also, if Molnar is correct, Our Lord was born on April 17, 6 CE. The Magi/Persian astrologers meet Joseph, Maryam and Jeshua in a house. In Matthew 2:12 the Greek word for the meeting place is *oikian*, which translates "house" in English. Our Christmas cards show the visit of the "Three Kings" in the stable, usually at the same time as the shepherds. The tradition in liturgical churches, of the Magi arriving twelve days later, is wiser and probably more accurate.

Whatever the case, the more important aspect to our story is that the Persians may have warned Joseph of Herod's mind. The two accounts are unclear here. The account in Matthew has Herod reacting almost immediately once he realizes that the Magi aren't going to report back to him. So Joseph is warned and flees to Egypt. The account in Luke has Joseph and Maryam and Jesus going to the Temple after forty days and then straight home to Nazareth. The timing is unclear here. The most logical scenario is that they fled to Egypt after the circumcision and returned to dedicate their son after Herod's death. The date of Herod's death is controversial, so it is difficult to pin this down. And we know another angelic dream confirms Joseph's suspicion, telling Joseph to clear out for Egypt.

So Joseph takes his little family and makes the journey to the Jewish community in Egypt, a left-over of the days when Jews fled to Egypt to escape the Babylonians.

At some point, Herod dies, and Joseph has another dream. So they return. It may have been the minimum forty days; it may have been longer. It's hard to believe it went the other way around, with Joseph suspecting that Herod wanted to kill them as he is heading toward the danger in Jerusalem. Perhaps Joseph at this point is hoping things will settle down and get mundane again.

Sorry Joseph. No luck there, pal.

Meditation Six: Maryam's Sword

SO JOSEPH IS TOLD in a dream that they can go home. But the presentation of the first-born male has to take place. This must have been nerve-wracking to Joseph, even with Herod dead. He is painfully aware of his foster-son's prophetic beginning and he knows Jesus is a target for the new rulers as well as the Romans. His best hope is that when they go to Jerusalem, no one will recognize them.

This is a vital moment for Maryam, so let me fully set the scene. After having spent their lives in tiny Nazareth, coming to Jerusalem must have been for them what coming to Manhattan would be to a boy that's never seen more than twenty miles past his Iowa farm. The noise and constant flow of people, all strangers, going in every direction, must have been astounding. The streets are not only full of people of every description, but market stalls, and the baying of cattle, the bleating of sheep, the startling smells of herbs and spices on display for sale. Maryam feels her senses are being overwhelmed. And the streets ran on and on like a maze. But the Temple is visible from all directions, rising into the sky, a large rectangular box shape jutting toward Heaven, dull white, looking like a refrigerator left by a giant, and open to the west with a large rectangular doorway. Concentric walls ring it round, and people flow like a river through the massive, open gates. Clouds of smoke rise from the courts where sacrifices are made. Voices cry out, braying above the crowd, praying loudly and formally.

Fortunately, Zechariah, has put them up for the night in his home with Elisheva and their son Johanan. Zechariah is off duty today and leads them through the streets to the Temple, through the massive gates, past the Court of the Gentiles, and makes sure that they get in the right line for presentation of infant boys. In front of them some twenty other young couples also hold small boys, some of which are squalling lustily. Joseph relaxes a little. They can blend in with this crowd. Zechariah wishes them luck and vanishes. He has much to do and the line will move slowly at best. He will see then back home for dinner. Joseph holds a cage with two turtledoves, the appointed sacrifice under the Law for a poor man to redeem his first-born son. This, and indeed their escape from Herod in Bethlehem, was all funded by selling the frankincense, and the myrrh, and spending the gold. The Persian astrologers had quite surprised her, and their gifts had seemed odd, but Yahweh provided and the gifts had made their whole journey possible. Without the gifts, their son would be dead and if they were alive, they would be in Herod's dungeons, never to emerge. The thought makes Maryam shiver.

Maryam too is nervous, aware of all the talk back in Bethlehem about the skies the night she gave birth and the way people had been looking at them there. As grateful as she was for Great-Uncle Levi's hospitality, she was glad to leave. Egypt was strange to her, staying a month in the Jewish colony there. Then Herod died suddenly. She silently thanked Yahweh, and her hope and faith are renewed.

Then there was the long, hot journey back to Judea up the dusty road, the strip of blue to the north being the only indication of the Mediterranean. Maryam, riding on her donkey, thought of Moses and the people who made this journey in ancient times. And with this thought, she looks down at the infant boy in her arms, wrapped up against the blazing sun, making all the little faces newborns make as their eyes slowly come in to focus. What is this in her arms? The visit from the archangel seems somehow distant. This little baby boy seems just another little baby boy. But deep in her heart, she knows that the donkey plodding step after dusty step is the illusion that the mundane gives us. Behind it all, Yahweh constantly works silently for the good of humanity in spite of the way they flaunt and ignore him. Yahweh is the earthquake under the soil, the thunder in the distance, and in the small cries of this helpless infant she cradles. Her mind tries to grasp all this and fails.

Now, as she and Joseph move up slowly in the line, she thinks the presentation will not last long. Tomorrow morning, they can bid farewell to Zechariah and Elisheva and begin the long-overdue journey home to Nazareth. She and her husband may be of the family of the ancient king, David, but they do not feel at home in Judah and haven't for some three or more generations. They speak with Galilean accents; they are foreigners here, even though they are Jews.

But as Maryam and Joseph reach the front of the line, the old man in white priest's garments looks at them and reaches out for the baby. Maryam surrenders the child reluctantly. But this old priest, his wisps of white hair

MEDITATION SIX: MARYAM'S SWORD

teasing out from under his priest's cap, he holds the child gently. At first he goes through all the prescribed words of the acceptance ceremony, accepting the boy for *Adonai*. Another younger priest takes the cage of turtledoves out of Joseph's hand, hands it to a third young priest, who takes it and three others off toward the blazing altar and the source of all the smoke. The words have been said, and Maryam gladly takes back her boy from the old man. But as she does so, he says loudly, so that a chill goes down her spine.

> *Adonai,* let your servant depart in peace
>
> According to your promise
>
> For my eyes have seen your salvation
>
> Which you fashioned in the sight of many nations
>
> A light of revelation to the Gentiles
>
> And a glory for your people, Israel.

Maryam is so startled that she is shaking, clutching her baby boy. The old man puts a hand on her arm and looks her directly in the eye, his face a hand's length away from hers.

"Beware, this child is set for the fall, . . . and the rising of many in Israel, and a sign that will be protested, that the thoughts of people's hearts will be revealed to the common day." Then in a voice barely above a whisper, the old priest said dark words that made Maryam shiver all the harder in her terror. "And a sword will pierce through your own soul as well." Then the old priest stepped back. Maryam almost turned and fled, only Joseph's hand on her arm keeping her from panic. You would think that would be enough. But as she turned, an old woman stood there, adoring the baby in Maryam's arms. The old woman loudly began thanking *Adonai* that the *Mashiach* had come. Between the old man and this old woman, there is no more hiding now. Everyone in the crowd has stopped talking and is staring at them. Joseph takes Maryam's arm and steers her out of the crowd, down the streets and back to Zechariah's house. Maryam makes the whole journey with her mind reeling in shock, clutching tight to her son, her face wet with her tears. This beautiful miracle of Yahweh had come to her and already people were shouting about her baby boy. They were going to take him away from her, she just knew, and her mind circled round and round in this fear, until she realized that Joseph had guided them safely back to Zechariah's and that Elisheva was helping her to the straw mattress where she and Joseph were sleeping during their stay. Elisheva stayed and soothed her until Maryam slept, not letting her baby boy an inch further from her breast that necessary.

I can feel some readers resisting my take on that day in the Temple. Every time this section of the Bible is read, it is read with something like a feeling of Christmas celebration. Joseph and Mary are just ecstatic over Simeon and Anna rejoicing over their son, who is the Messiah. I think we are tempted to project ourselves into that crowd that was in the Temple that day.

"Jesus the Messiah is here! Hallelujah! Everything is going to be great now! Merry Christmas!"

But if we go back with the Ghost of Christmas Past to the actual date, such a thing could not have been. Joseph, Maryam, and Jeshua were not surrounded by American Christians celebrating. They were surrounded by first-century Jews, to whom the word *Mashiach* was a cause for deep concern and even fear. Simeon and Anna could see deeper and further; the crowd most certainly could not.

Certainly Maryam and Joseph know that the birth of this son, conceived in such a startling and supernatural way, was something big and special. But they had no way of knowing what. They had no way of knowing at that point that the crucifixion would be followed by the Resurrection. All these things would have been mind-blowing to them. And all they had to go on was the accepted notion in their time that the Messiah (*Mashiach*) would be a military and political figure, something Jesus of Nazareth tried very hard to play down when his time actually came. And messiah candidates had appeared before and raised followings, usually only to end up dead at Roman hands. Not only were their fellow Jews hypersensitive to any claims that this or that person was the Messiah, but so were the Romans. In the end, this was Pilate's justification for crucifying Jesus of Nazareth, Maryam's son: because he just might be another one of those bothersome Jewish messiahs that challenged Caesar.

So imagine Maryam, hearing these prophecies about her helpless, precious little babe in arms. It would have sounded like a death sentence to her. Indeed, as Simeon promised, a sword did pierce her soul—again, and again, and again.

She must have feared. But I have said that I believed her to have then and now, an unusual grace, a holiness not of her own making. And I suppose much of the ever-virgin-Buddha poses of Mary in art are meant to portray this state of holiness, as if it somehow puts her above pain and

MEDITATION SIX: MARYAM'S SWORD

suffering, and indeed, above all human emotion. Nonsense. That's more a Buddhist concept than a Christian one.

If I may paraphrase the Apostle Paul, I believe for Maryam, she experienced fear, but she did not let the sun go down on it. We all are struck by our emotions. Sin involves the will, the choices made after the first reaction. I believe that Maryam may have gone to sleep in fear, but when she woke, calmed down, she decided that Yahweh was not going to be side-tracked by prophecies or Roman governments, and that she, Maryam of Nazareth, would wait and see how this was all to play out. That's what, in that particular moment, holiness looked like.

Why do I think this?

Because it's what her Son did in the Garden of Gethsemane. His fear caused him to ask the cup to be removed, but he thought better of it and decided to trust God instead.[1] If Jesus is the Son of God, then holiness looks like the actions and choices of Jesus, not like a Buddha pose floating effortlessly above the pains and concerns of the world.

The Biblical account says that Maryam pondered all these things in her heart. I'm sure she did.

Then nothing happened.

That's right. Nothing happened for a long time, twelve years to be exact. At least that's the way the Bible tells it.

I don't believe that either. Why? Because we know that Jesus, years later, went through his thirteenth to his thirtieth years, a grand total of seventeen years as an adult male by all the standards of his time, and he just worked with Joseph and lived with his parents. As a novelist myself I know that when you tell a story, you weave the narrative around the high points. We as viewers of video, are far more impatient than our recent ancestors, who were only impatient about what they were reading. "Cut to the chase!" we cry. There is no chase when you spend twenty years in domestic routine, nor even in forty days praying in a desert. Sure, Christ was tempted in the desert, but those three exchanges with Satan took minutes. Most of the forty days he was experiencing a prolonged fast in harsh conditions. In the desert, even with sufficient food and water, your whole mind is turned to emptying itself and listening, overcoming your loud and persistent appetites, which is counter-intuitive to humans, and is even more so in the age of instant gratification we live in now. And there was a flowering of strange Infancy Narratives about Jesus that did just that, in which he is a rather

1. Matthew 26:39

mean-spirited little miracle worker. The church has never taken these, such as "The Gospel of Thomas" seriously, but sadly they come from the same Gnostic impulses that gave birth to the Gospel of James.

My point is, we want to fill in that gap of twelve years of childhood, just as Gnostic writers did in their so-called gospels. Impatient as we are, we want our own narratives to be one mountaintop experience after another. But our God is a God of the valleys as well. God is with us in the mundane, or the silent, or the agonizing, just as he is in the moments of celebration or triumph, or even in the moments of drama. That isn't nothing happening; that is quiet and vital development.

Think about it. We know Our Lord's ministry lasted roughly three years and he died and rose in around his thirty-third year of human life. That means that for a grand total of thirty years of his life on Earth, 91% of it, he quietly waited. Nothing happened, at least not by our action and adventure standards. And recall that for a boy to turn thirteen was to enter manhood. Your thirties were middle-age. Anyone forty or older was an old man or an old woman. Almost nobody reached 50, much less 60. Luke's Gospel says Anna was 84, but the point of that was that she was waiting to see the Messiah, and so lived an extraordinarily long life. It would be for us like someone living to 120 just to see Jesus. Simeon, most likely, was not quite so old. He may well have been in his forties.

So Our Lord spent his young manhood being a Nazareth *tekton*, never marrying and starting his amazing ministry in middle age. We think of him as cut off in his youth, being executed by the Romans at 33, but for the Jews of the time, that was a pretty long life, 33.

But let us return to Joseph and Maryam making their way north to Nazareth. When they arrive at Heli's home, their home, Jacob and Jeremiah are there working the farm together. Joseph and Maryam have been gone almost three months. Jacob tells his sister that Heli was struck with some kind of paralysis on the left side of his body and just quietly passed away. They have no name for this thing. Today, we call it a stroke. Thus the homecoming is sad. One more sword goes through Maryam's soul, but it won't be the last. Jacob and Jeremiah meet their new nephew, which is a small spot of joy. Life resumes. Joseph goes to Sepphoris the next day to work. Maryam cooks, cleans, and nurses her child. Mundane living returns.

In a year, Jacob marries and Joseph builds Maryam their own house in town. There the growing boy, Jeshua (Jesus in the Greek) grows up learning from Joseph all the skills with wood, metal, and stone that Joseph knows.

And, for seventeen years, nothing happens.

But it does. It is just in God's economy, these things aren't nothing—living in a tough existence, working with the people around you day to day, loving the people close to you who have irritated you too many times, and living quietly enough to hear God's whispering. God doesn't write the kind of novel of our lives that we would prefer. He writes a lot of "slow" passages, and we tend to think our life is off the track. The hardest thing in the world, for many people, including me, is to quietly wait for something promised.

But this growing boy, Jesus of Nazareth, knew that his life was not off track even if he had no adventures bigger than looking for lost sheep. Maryam looks at him, remembering the startling way he was born, and the prophecies which still trouble her. He is a good boy, kind, patient, and mature far beyond his years. She stops her work for a moment, stands in the door of her house and watches him from a distance, guiding the small flock of sheep out to pasture with their dog.

There is a scene in the classic movie, *Ben Hur*, in which Judah ben Hur is a Roman prisoner being marched to the galleys, chained to other prisoners. The Roman NCO in charge takes a disliking to him and decides that Judah doesn't get water. They stop at a village to water the prisoners, all but Judah. Unexpectedly, a young man, whose face we never see, gives water to Judah ben Hur. Of course we all know that the young man in Jesus of Nazareth, the Christ. The NCO starts to light in to this interfering local, but when he sees the young man's face, he falls silent.

That is a fictional movie scene, but I suspect something like this happened and more than once. That weird kid, that son of Joseph was likely to do something crazy like that, helping Roman prisoners or going out of his way to help a neighbor. And he was like that as a young man, and before that as a boy. And I strongly suspect that his mother, Maryam, was like that too. I can see that same *Ben Hur* scene with the NCO cowed to silence by the look in the face of Maryam of Nazareth, as she gives water to Roman prisoners. She may have been a woman in a patriarchal society, but she was not easily put off when she knew something was right. Call it boldness if you like, this girl who made up a song about the rich being sent away empty.

Or, like me, you can call it the grace of holiness.

Meditation Seven: Just When You Thought Nothing Would Ever Change

AND SO THE YEARS roll on. Three years after Jesus, Jacob (I'll call him James by his Greek name to avoid confusion), is born and Jesus becomes a big brother, leading his little brother around as they watch Uncle Jacob's sheep. Two years after that, Dvorah is born, named after Maryam's beloved cousin who died a young woman of some unknown and severe pain in her abdomen. Appendicitis was always fatal in the first century. Two years later came Joseph, and Judah, twins and the first named for his father. Jesus leads a flock of little brothers and sister around, and they also work at Uncle Jacob's farm because that's what families do, and Jacob has had no children. Maryam's brother Jeremiah has built a house nearby, and he and Joseph are trying to pick up all the building business in Nazareth. Jeremiah's wife has had nothing but girls, and Jeremiah appreciates the way that his nephews Jesus and James work well in the shop. Joseph jr and Judah are still too small.

Maryam becomes pregnant again in short order, birthing two more girls, Elisheva and Ana a year apart. They are named for her dear mother and her dear cousin. And two years later little Shimon is born. By this time, Maryam is much older and feeling the effects on her body of eight children. At 24 years of age she can feel middle age approaching. She is nothing like the lithe, slender girl she once was. Her breasts, once small, have now suckled eight children and her hips are wide from the passage of multiple babies. But she is not fat, even by our standards today in the post-Twiggy age. Being fat is a luxury for people like Lucius, who feast with the Romans until they are no longer hungry. Maryam and Joseph and their family have never once in their life eaten a meal and stopped feeling hungry, with the exception of perhaps wedding feasts. There simply isn't enough money and enough food, even with brother Jacob quietly slipping them grain he owes to his master, Lucius. They have never had a meal in their life in which they stopped eating because they were no longer hungry, never known a meal that didn't end with the hunger pains still crying from their bellies.

SEVEN: JUST WHEN YOU THOUGHT NOTHING WOULD EVER CHANGE

Such a thing is luxury beyond imagination for them, only to come when the community came together for a wedding. In addition, with all the hard years of labor, at almost ;middle age, 24 years old, aches and muscle pains now attend Maryam in her daily work. Fortunately, ten-year-old Dvorah is proving to be an excellent helper and eldest daughter, sharing mother duties as is the tendency in large families.

Jesus of Nazareth, Our Lord, spent his ministry surrounded by men whom he'd chosen that in some sense were like little brothers to his leading. It seems to me immensely possible that the place Our Lord learned this model was within his own family.

For Maryam, though she remembers the archangel's visit and the extraordinary events around her eldest son's birth, all that seems so far in the past now. She really can't be blamed for thinking, and to be honest, hoping that maybe the prophecies swirling around her son are something different and quieter than what she feared. And usually, it's when we fall in to such a complacency that God likes to surprise us. Especially if one is as impatient as I am, it's very easy once things settle into a routine, to expect that change has left forever. And then something explodes, and we lose our footing.

One high point of the year is the way that the entire Jewish nation, save those too poor or ill to travel, or unable to leave their farms, would go to Jerusalem for the high holy day of the Passover. Maryam and Joseph have gone most years, except when childbirth or illness or advanced age has prevented. It has been at least five years since the last time, and they've never before taken the children. The little ones stayed with Aunt Rachel last time. Spring is coming and Jeshua (Jesus) will see his twelfth year. Next spring after this one, he will stand up and read the introduction to the reading of the Torah in the synagogue. He will be a man. And Maryam, for all the quiet years, has a sense that something will happen after that. The archangel said he was the Son of God, the *Mashiach*. What would that feel like? Imagine that you knew beforehand that your child was going to be President of the United States and die by assassination. Imagine what a lump in your throat you'd get every time you let your mind touch this knowledge. Maryam doesn't know how this will play out, but if the miraculous events were an indication, things would not go quietly for her son, Jesus, once he became a man. And she struggles with one other thought: the way the archangel talked about Jesus at his conception, he spoke of him as the Son of God, and as if this boy were Yahweh himself come to visit. She looks into the workshop where Jesus is chipping stone with a chisel.

Jesus doesn't look up. This boy, who tells her so sweetly "Yes, Mama" when she asks him to do anything, this boy, this boy . . . is Yahweh himself? Her mind puzzles. Passover is coming up. It has been years since they were able to make the journey to Jerusalem. Money has been tight. But last year, Joseph got extra work. They should go. What would happen when this boy, her dear, dear eldest son, saw Jerusalem?

Joseph wants to take the oldest children to Jerusalem this year, Jesus, James, and Dvorah. They will leave the twins, the other two girls and Shimon with Jacob and his wife, who love the children all the more since they cannot have children of their own. Jacob, Maryam's brother, is especially fond of little Joseph, Judah, and Shimon. And Maryam hopes that he'll make one of them his heir and pass on the farm to them. So it is all agreed. A large party of the family is going, even elderly Aunt Rachel, almost 50 years old and the matriarch of the clan. They will all travel together to Jerusalem for Passover.

While the family is preparing for the journey, I want to explore something that I've only touched on lightly till now. As I've said, the guiding principle that I'm building this meditation on is that Jesus is like Mary because Mary is like Jesus. And if you're a Christian at all, you have to believe that Jesus was the Holy Son of God. I have argued that Maryam herself partakes of this holiness to some degree and in some fashion, though I am reluctant to label it with something formulaic like "immaculate conception."

But the question arises: what does holiness look like? I've touched lightly on an answer three times now. I have argued that what it *does not* look like is this untouchable Buddha-meditation state that European art has traditionally used since the beginning of painting Jesus and Mary as icons in the Byzantine culture. And I've given a clue in my allusion to the scene from the movie, *Ben Hur*, in which Christ gives water to a prisoner in need in spite of Roman opposition. And I've argued that Christ's vast empathy was shared by his mother, Maryam.

But I am not going to attempt to define holiness. And I don't really need to: Jesus has already done so, across the breadth of the Gospels:

Be poor in spirit, and the kingdom of heaven is yours. Blessed are those who mourn, for they will be comforted. Blessed are the meek, a word we now confuse. The meek are those, who like doctors, "do no harm". They will inherit the earth. Thirst for righteousness, and you will be filled. Be merciful, and you will be shown mercy. Be pure in heart, that is, single-mindedly loving him above all else, and you will see God. Be the peacemaker, and you will be called children of God. Blessed are those who are persecuted because of righteousness, for theirs is the kingdom of heaven. Blessed are you when people insult you, persecute you and falsely say all kinds of evil against you because of Christ. Rejoice and be glad, because great is your reward in heaven, for in the same way they persecuted the prophets who were before you.

That's Matthew's take in his chapter 5. Luke in chapter 8 adds: Blessed are you who are poor, for yours is the kingdom of God. Blessed are you who hunger now, for you will be satisfied. Blessed are you who weep now, for you will laugh. Right there all the things which anchor our sense of individualism have just been undermined by Christ. But it goes on: Blessed are you when people hate you, when they exclude you and insult you and reject your name as evil, because of the Son of Man. And we can keep touring the Gospels and find more. Forgive if you want to be forgiven. Love your enemy. If your enemy strikes you, turn the other cheek. Visit prisoners. Feed the hungry. Clothe the naked. Do not put your trust in riches, nor worship Mammon. I've only scratched the surface here.

The thing we never seem to get is that holiness is about what you do, not what you don't do. Worrying about what not to do, that is, avoiding sins, and spending time trying to get other people to avoid sins, that's Puritanism. Jesus rarely spoke in thou shalt nots; he spoke in "Blessed is" and "do thou likewise."

Fine, you the reader say, you've heard all this before, read out in church week after week. And yet, when I went to define holiness, I'm guessing that you were expecting some other answer. We should know this by now, but we don't. Paul Simon was right when he sang in his song, "The Boxer" "A man hears what he wants to hear and disregards the rest."

But, you the reader say, this is all really idealized stuff. Nobody could live like this in reality.

Jesus did.

And yes, I think he expects his followers to try to do so as well, as hard as that may be. And I think Mary did. Was her holiness some glowing zen-state of detachment from the world? I cannot believe that. I believe Maryam of Nazareth was given a grace to live what her son teaches. That is her holiness, her immaculate conception. I think the tendency in art and thought, to try and picture holiness as detachment is 180 degrees backwards. Holiness can be burned down to Jesus' best-known sound bite:

1. Love Yahweh with your heart, mind, and soul
2. Love your neighbor as yourself

Then he added that on these two commandments depend all the law and the prophets.[1] And both are things to do, not things not to do.

Everything listed above from the Gospels burns down to that. Love God with everything you've got. Love your neighbor like you love yourself. Neither of those is detached. They are both focused outward. Yes, yes, I recognize the value of meditation, especially in quieting the mind to better hear God's whispers. But that is a means, not an end. The end is to give ourselves away to God and neighbor. That is holiness. That is what Jesus lived. And that is what his mother lived.

This is a great stumbling stone and most people have heard it a thousand times and are still deaf to it. I believe that vast majority of humanity is really of one religion, and it isn't Christianity. It's what I call the Religion of Luck. We can't hear Jesus in Matthew 22 because it contradicts our real faith, the Religion of Luck.

I was in Shanghai, China last summer and my daughter and son-in-law took me to visit a temple. In the temple, people were placing offerings to ask these gods for luck: they wanted health, or a job, or some other form of success and prosperity. This is very much a part of Chinese and indeed, all east-Asian culture. But I don't think it's limited to east Asia. Here in America, we don't really love God above all else, because that would get in the way of our comfortable, middle-class lives. We prefer to keep God at a comfortable distance. We like him at arm's length, there in case of emergencies that threaten our comfortable lives. He is our divine fire-extinguisher.

And we don't love our neighbor as ourselves because that would be awkward and expensive. And besides, here in American culture, we have a value that we hold far more highly than the two the Christ puts first: we believe in individualism above all else. I can't love my neighbor as myself if he's in trouble, because I earned mine and he can just go out and earn his and leave me alone. "A man hears what he wants to hear and disregards the rest."

We are deaf to Christ.

But his mother, I believe, wasn't. That's the difference between her and us. And I am pleased to say that I've met many people who aren't deaf. But they tend to be fewer than one would hope. She was given a grace, an ability

---

1. Matthew 22:35-40

SEVEN: JUST WHEN YOU THOUGHT NOTHING WOULD EVER CHANGE

beyond her own from God. It strikes me that though you and I aren't immaculately conceived, we too can ask for some of that grace.

But let's watch the clan leaving Nazareth, Joseph and Jeremiah in the lead, Aunt Rachel on her donkey not far behind, and followed by the women like Maryam, surrounded by their brothers and sisters and aunts and uncles and cousins, as well as their children. Our Lord was not without family, even if you believe him to have been an only child. Twelve-year-old Jesus of Nazareth walks quietly in the midst of the group, not far from his mother. For three days they trek around the east coast of the Sea of Galilee and then due south, avoiding the direct route through Samaria, even if that is shorter. Jews don't talk to half-breed Samaritans.

Once they reach Jerusalem, they stay with Cousin Zechariah and Cousin Elisheva, and their son, now thirteen and just become a man, young Johanan ben Zechariah. Some of the family stays in the stable, but not Maryam, Joseph, and the children this time. The next day the Passover begins and the family is gathered in the main room for the sacred meal. Maryam is sitting with Joseph on her left and Jesus on her right hand side.

She is trying to concentrate on the Seder, on Zechariah, now the family patriarch and his words, but her mind wanders.

Zechariah prays "Blessed are You, Lord our God, King of the Universe, who creates the fruit of the vine. We thank you God for giving us the gift of Festivals for joy and holidays for happiness, among them this day of Passover, the festival of our liberation, a day of sacred assembly recalling the Exodus from Egypt. Blessed are You, Lord our God, King of the universe, who has kept us in life, sustained us, and enabled us to reach this season."

The hand-washing, dipping of the herbs in salt water, and the breaking of the *matzah*, the unleavened bread, pass before her. Then it is the first turn for her second son, James, to speak. He is the youngest boy in the room.

"Why is this night different from all other nights?" he asks on cue.

The rest of the family answers in a stumbling unison: "We were slaves to Pharaoh in Egypt, and God brought us out with a strong hand and an outstretched arm. And if God had not brought our ancestors out of Egypt, we and our children and our children's children would still be subjugated to Pharaoh in Egypt."

And Maryam's mind is reeling back to their own short exile in Egypt, after Jesus was born. They too were called forth from Egypt. A coincidence? She looks at Jesus sitting next to her and watches him for some time. He is focused on the words of the ritual. She cannot forget the visit of the archangel and the ominous words of prophecy. She has an almost overpowering urge to wrap her arms around him to protect him. Only the embarrassment it would cause for her to fairly rise from her bench and embrace him stops her from carrying out the urge.

Her mind ricochets into another direction. We were slaves to Pharaoh. We are still slaves, but to Caesar now. Will it ever end? Is this son of mine the beginning of the end of this chain of slaveries?

The blessing is said and with bitter herbs the meal commences. Soft conversation starts around the table, and Maryam realizes that Jesus is now holding her gaze and looking back at her.

"What is it, Mama?"

"Oh, Jeshua, you are growing up so fast, I . . ."

"Don't be afraid, Mama," he says, and Maryam is startled by the calm reassurance in his voice, and by the way that her son seems to read her very fears and hear her thoughts. Maryam feels her heart racing, but as her son smiles at her, she feels calmer and her fears fade slowly. She reaches over and caresses his face.

The meal proceeds on to the dessert and the wine. Aunt Rachel must go out to the privy to relieve herself, but she can barely walk, her joints are now so stiff from years of hard labor. Young Johanan, Zechariah's son, a strapping, strong young man now of thirteen, rises and assists the elder lady out of the room.

After the last cup of wine is set out for the prophet, James' final job comes. Zechariah asks him to go to the door and see if Elijah has come. He opens the door and his cousin Johanan is standing there, holding the hand of Aunt Rachel. This has never happened before; normally the doorstep is empty when the child opens the door. Everyone is startled. Some of the people at the table gasp and others snicker, before suppressing their laughter on this holy day. Johanan looks embarrassed, but says nothing, leading the elder lady in and helping her to her bench, before returning to his own.

They sing: "Elijah the Prophet, Elijah the Tishbite, Elijah the Giladite, may he come speedily to us in our days along with Messiah the son of David." Maryam looks at Jesus. He smiles back at her but continues to sing with the others. As the night grows old, Maryam finds herself exhausted, emotionally and physically. She must be getting old. She excuses herself and goes to bed early. Tomorrow will be a big day. They will visit the Temple of Yahweh.

SEVEN: JUST WHEN YOU THOUGHT NOTHING WOULD EVER CHANGE

Though Maryam has been here several times since that day that Simeon and Anna zinged them with prophecy, Maryam cannot forget that startling day. The Temple is the same: huge with multiple concentric courtyards of high stone walls circling the vast standing rectangle. The crowds push and shove and the hubbub of voices overwhelms any attempt to talk at a low volume. The cry of dying animals and the smoke of incessant burning flesh pours out of the central courtyard. Maryam cannot remember a larger mob pushing and shoving. Getting around takes a long time, most of it moving slowly in lines. She begins to long for it to be over so they can begin their first day's journey north to quiet Nazareth and home. Mostly she's focused on Aunt Rachel, who maneuvers with difficulty in the crowds and keeping little Dvorah firmly by one hand. Joseph and Jeremiah and the others are watching the older children, Jesus and James.

So when Joseph leads them back out of the Temple, up the streets and out the gate, Maryam is relieved, breathing freely. They get Aunt Rachel on her donkey and out onto the road and it's almost an hour before Maryam, weary already in the mid-morning, starts looking around the family group now that they're not shoving through the crowds. They are all shuffling up the dusty road in the late morning. She spots James, bringing up the rear, which is typical of him. Her hand is firmly in Dvorah's hand. Someone is missing. She starts to panic as she looks around.

"Stop! Joseph, stop!"

He stops and everyone stumbles to a halt.

"Where's Jesus?"

Joseph and Jeremiah begin looking around. Maryam can feel panic rising. My son, my son. Where is my son?

Jeremiah says he will take the rest of the family as well as Dvorah and James to the inn where they plan to stop the first night. Joseph and Maryam turn and begin a much faster walk back to Jerusalem. They hope to meet at the inn later tonight.

Where did you last see him? I don't know. Where did *you* last see him? He was in the Temple with us, I know. I don't remember seeing him as we left the city. Let's start at the Temple.

After a terse hour searching the Temple they accidentally stumble into a group of scribes, in their official robes, discussing in a circle. Joseph says "Maybe they've seen him."

Maryam is startled when the circle of finely-robed scribes opens up and there is Jesus in the middle of them and in the middle of their discussion.

Maryam's anger flares "Son! Come! We are leaving."

Jesus gets up and walks with them away from the group of Scribes, who watch them go, as Maryam hears one of two of them say, "That child, his remarks were so well thought out. Amazing in a peasant boy."

Once they are outside the gates, Maryam's anger fades and she puts her arm around Jesus' shoulder. "Son, you frightened us. We were looking for you everywhere."

He looks up at her, suddenly not a child, with a look that makes him look like some stranger that she doesn't know.

"Didn't you know that I would be in my Father's house?"

The words hit Maryam like a flying stone. Yes, she thinks to herself, I was beginning to think of you as just my boy, just another boy in Nazareth. The slow years have lulled my sense of miracle to sleep. I should not forget again. The archangel brought me this boy.

She looks at Joseph, who looks as stunned as she feels.

What are they in for?

Meditation Eight: Another Lull

AND THEN TWENTY YEARS slid by. Jesus returned with them to Nazareth, read in the synagogue and became a man. He then showed no interest in taking a wife. He worked with his father as a *tekton*, going off to Sepphoris in the mornings. Life goes on, day after day much the same. She rises, bakes bread, feeds everyone, cleans, bakes more, cleans the house, provides dinner. Then she goes out and watches stars. What changes is the children growing up and the old passing away. And children have children of their own. Aunt Rachel passed away at last. By her thirty-fifth birthday, Maryam finds herself to be the matriarch of the family. Her joints too are getting stiffer, but she does not let up. A young man asks for Dvorah's hand and there was a wedding. James and Jesus continue to help Joseph and Jeremiah. Brother Jacob has adopted Joseph junior and Judah. They will together inherit his farm. Elisheva and Ana now help their mother and Shimon approaches his day of manhood in the synagogue. If I were to select a song to sum up Maryam's life, it would be "Sunrise, Sunset" from *Fiddler on the Roof*.

After the shock in the Temple, Maryam expected there to be something remarkable happening with Jesus. But he acts as if he is just another poor young man of Nazareth. Still, Maryam knows that something is coming. Yahweh's timing is somehow slow. Who knows what he is thinking? Perhaps Jesus does, but he does not say a word about his sense of who he is.

Then the very worst happens. Jesus and Jeremiah come home one day leading a cart pulled by a donkey. On the bed of the cart is a body wrapped in a dull white shroud. A stone wall fell and Joseph is crushed. Maryam stands in the road in front of her house listening to a voice that sounds like her brother's voice, telling her that her dear Joseph is dead. She rocks as the earth shakes. Jesus comes over and holds her. They ask her if she wants them to unwrap the body around the head, so that she can say farewell. She shakes her head no. She wants to remember him alive and well, not crushed and bloody. He is buried swiftly and honorably, as is the custom. Maryam's heart is crushed. The wall that has fallen on Joseph has fallen on her as well. Though she married him out of practicality, she has come to love him so much over the years. Her empty bed yawns like a cave. It is months before she can make it through a day without tears. The sword has pierced her soul again.

For those who see a celibate Maryam, you've got her now. As a widow not too old, most people expect her to remarry. She shows no interest. This is not because she thinks celibacy a holier state; this is because no one could come close to Joseph in her heart, ever. She has her sons, her daughters and her hope. She does not need a husband.

Jesus now works with his uncle to bring in the small amounts of money that keep them from starving, with James and Shimon following him around. James finds a bride and brings her home. They build a new room for James and his wife, who is named Ruth. Shimon reads in the synagogue and all her sons are grown now. Elisheva, named for her dear cousin who also passed two years back, has an offer of marriage and now it's just Ana and Ruth in the kitchen with Maryam most days. They do all they can to relieve her of tasks, but she still has a lot of work. Yet it does allow her to take breaks and walk out the back door to see the beauty of the day or the beauty of the stars. No one will stop her; she is the matriarch and has earned the privilege of quiet time.

Their home is well-known in town. Beggars frequent it, standing at the door fully confident they will get a piece of bread. Anyone in town who needs a supportive ear to listen knows that Maryam's heart is wide and her patience is deep. The hungry go there, even though Jesus and James earn barely enough bread for the family. They are never turned away.

Elisheva, her cousin, passed away as did Zechariah. But cousin Johanan did not don the robes of a Levite like his father. Reports are that he has wandered off to live in the desert like a prophet from the writings. No one knows where he is. When Maryam hears it, she looks at Jesus, wondering. But he continues to work.

At last, after years of silence, they are both standing out watching the stars arriving as sundown fades. Maryam speaks, "My son. Have you heard about your cousin Johanan?"

"Yes, mother."

"And you?"

He turns and looks at her.

"You know your gift," she says. "I mean, . . . well, I just don't know what to expect. You are not like the others, not like anyone. You . . . ." She cannot finish her sentence.

He's still looking at her but it's so dark she really cannot see his face. He says very quietly. "It's not time yet, mother."

"But when, . . . ?"

"When it is time, I will know. You will know."

They both fall silent. But Maryam has set her face, even here with her son. "It has been over ten years since we found you in the Temple. We have never spoken of it."

He doesn't answer. He has already told her all that she can be told. When it's time, she will know and so will he. She is unhappy with this, but she remembers how in everything so far *Adonai* has had his own timing. Abraham had to wait, as had Moses. She lets out her breath and her shoulders sag. She has trusted *Adonai* this far. And that's where her holiness leaves most of us behind. We are really good at wallowing in doubts, at least I am. Doubts hit everyone, even Jesus in the Garden of Gethsemane. But he did not let his sun set on them, to paraphrase Paul. Nor did his mother.

But all families have tensions. And I think we have to realize that Our Lord had folks. Even if you hold that Jesus was an only child, he had through his mother, uncles, aunts, and cousins. We know about John the Baptist. Those who believe James and the other brothers and sisters were really cousins, have to own this. And one thing this means is that though it's not like the Dan Brown fantasy where Jesus has children by Mary Magdalene that live and breath today, it does mean that Jesus has cousins, nieces, and nephews, genetically speaking, and many generations removed, that live and breathe today. Outside of those of us who have entered God's family by faith, there are those who share some of his DNA if we could trace it. This fact probably makes us think of all sorts of possibilities; but there again, most of what we might dream of is a projection of a Jesus and a Mary that look and think like our own culture. The thought that comes to me is that some of these distant physical cousins to Jesus of Nazareth died in the Holocaust.

But back to the first century and the family. Jesus, now tall, with long, dark hair and beard, works steadily in the shop or at Sepphoris as there is work. Uncle Jeremiah works there as well, and James does too, but James is often irritated by Jesus. Why does big brother get this almost awed attitude from our mother? Why hasn't he married? Why does he seem, year after year, to be waiting for something? James gets angry at Jesus sometimes, but Jesus stays calm. If James apologizes, Jesus always forgives.

James in the meantime has had two sons by Ruth, though sadly, the birth of the second son was too much for her and she died a week later. Sadness drapes like a shroud over the house again, and Maryam feels the sword pierce her soul one more time. Ana has an offer of marriage, but turns it down. Jesus won't force her, as is his right as male head of household. She wants to stay close to her mother. Maryam urges her to reconsider, but is secretly grateful when Ana "sets her face" and refuses to leave. Must be a family trait. And Maryam delights in Zechariah and Elisha, her two grandsons by James. Shimon soon finds a bride and moves into his father-in-law's house. Elisheva has three daughters and stops bearing. She names them Maryam, Ana, and Dvorah. So Maryam has five grandchildren whom she adores, including a little name-sake. She volunteers to watch them as often as possible. Maryam feels the whole world has changed. She stands on the edge as eldest while the young generation plays at her feet.

And still Jesus does not marry, nor does he seem to change.

His years of his twenties come and go. At thirty, he enters middle age, still a bachelor, still working as a *tekton*. Maryam wonders. When it's time, they will know. She does wonder if *Adonai* has forgotten, but then she doesn't think this for long. She knows better. Her faith is ocean-deep. Some years ago I found a movie on the life of Mary titled *Mary of Nazareth*. The film was produced by a Catholic publisher and has a Catholic point of view, and it does quite a few things well. Of course, there are problems. The pretty German actress, Alyssa Jung, plays Mary, even though she looks thoroughly Caucasian. Still, as the movie proceeds, she does a good job of portraying Maryam as a woman of faith in a very perplexing situation where she does not see what God is doing. There are some racy plot elements involving Spanish actress, Paz Vega, as Mary Magdalene. But in spite of the superior acting of Jung, certain elements betray that this film too is more a mirror than a window. I won't even talk about the ever-virgin issue here. Beyond that and the fact that Maryam is Caucasian, she doesn't age. Jesus goes off one day on his ministry, looking about 20 years old. She looks more like his sister than his mother. The make-up people did their best, but only time will make this pretty German actress look older.

And these are the elements of our mirror-illusion about Maryam of Nazareth: one, the ever-virginity; two, the seeing her as somehow floating in a holy Buddha-meditation state all her life; and three, seeing her as always about 20 years old, even when her son was older than that.

If Jesus left home to begin his ministry in his thirtieth year, Maryam was at least 43 years old. This was, in the short-lived, medically almost ignorant times they lived in, early old age. The Maryam that finally sends her son into the world is an old woman.

The moment comes unexpectedly, of course. God is the God of surprises. Maryam is standing outside the back door, looking down into brother Jacob's fields as the sun sets. She sees the silhouettes of her two sons, Joseph and Judah, a quarter of a mile away, digging in the field. Then Jesus is there, standing beside her. They do not talk until it is completely dark, silently enjoying the beauty of *Adonai's* sunset together. She feels something in her heart rising. She is not sure whether it's fear or joy. It is like a great weight inside her, or maybe something that wants to explode. Then she knows.

"It's time, isn't it?" she says simply.

"Yes. I will go in the morning."

"Son?"

"Yes?"

"Please hold me."

She hugs her son for a very long time. It could be the last. No one knows the will of *Adonai*.

In the morning, he is gone with the rising sun. James is annoyed. "We really could have used his help. Where did he say he was going?"

Maryam just looks out the front door down the dusty road.

Meditation Nine: The Storm Arrives

For several weeks there is nothing and Maryam wonders what is happening. When it does happen, it is not pleasant.

"Maryam! I hear your son is going around the country preaching. And he has followers! Can you imagine?"

"Maryam! They say your son thinks he's the messiah! Can you believe it?"

"Maryam! I am so sorry to hear that your son has gone crazy."

Maryam keeps a lid on her anger for some of this. No one knows what *Adonai* is doing. It doesn't help that James gets irritated at each piece of gossip and flies into a litany of complaints about his big brother. But Maryam knows that James is worried sick, and hurt that Jesus left with having said so little and having explained nothing. Maryam knows that all of James' blame of Jesus is at heart his love for his brother frustrated. The family life moves on. Little Zechariah and Elisha are growing up and call Ana "*amtah*", or "aunt" in Aramaic. Yet, she has become their mother in every other respect.

Then after some long months of listening to gossip, Maryam's heart leaps up because the eldest of Elisheva's daughters, her namesake, little Maryam, now grown to a girl of 13, is to marry a man of Cana, a town just ten miles up the road past Sepphoris to the north. They are to go, being family, and Maryam is told that Jesus passed through Cana, was told, and assured his niece that he would also attend. All of this is wonderful, the marriage of a grandchild and the chance for a trip, but none of that makes her heart leap like a chance to see her son, now that . . . now that he's . . . . Maryam can't think what to call Jesus' new phase.

Then she hears about cousin Johanan, calling people to repentance and baptizing in the River Jordan. The temperature of her anxiety goes up a notch. Things are starting to happen. She hears that even her Jesus was baptized by his cousin.

None of this dims the bubbling in her heart as with Jeremiah, his wife and daughters, Ana and the children, Judah, Joseph, Shimon and his wife, the family sets out. James has found a donkey for Maryam to ride and leads the creature. Maryam's joints aren't what they used to be and she's grateful. By mid-morning they come up the dusty roads and find their way through the gaudy stone Roman buildings of Sepphoris. Maryam cannot take her eyes off the splendid buildings. But she does not see splendor. She sees a wall fall and the only man she ever loved, destroyed. Could Joseph have been saved by her son's power? And if so, why didn't he? But these are the kinds of questions that *Adonai* never answers. And something in her she could never explain absolutely trusts *Adonai*. She watches her donkey pick her way across the carefully laid brick road. To her left a string of columns seems to hold a roof floating in air. To her right down a hill there is an amphitheater, something Joseph had told her about as he worked on it. Though she was curious to see it, she is glad when the last of Sepphoris drops away behind her. And she's grateful they did not run into Lucius and have to bow and scrape to him.

By mid-afternoon they arrive in the next village, which is Cana, looking not all that different than Nazareth—pokey little houses clustered together around a small square with a few tradesmen's shops. They stop at a house looking much like her own: an outer wall enclosing a large open-air, central living space with rooms built along the wall inside and one roofed corner designated for cooking. But unlike Maryam's home, this house is crammed with people, of whom Maryam knows few. Tables are set up with a head table running perpendicular to five long tables covering much of the dirt courtyard. Maryam's eyes are looking everywhere, and she can't help herself when she sees Jesus in the crowd. She slips off her donkey and runs to him as much as with her stiff joints she can run, crashes into him and wraps her arms around him, holding him for quite some time. When she lets him go, he introduces her to the six men standing around him, smiling. The big tall one with chaotically curly hair and beard is Shimon, though Jesus calls him Petros. The shorter one that looks like Petros is his brother, with a very Aramaic, or perhaps Greek name, Andraus. There are two sons of Zebediah, Jacob and Johanan, the first a tall man with a round face who says he prefers the Greek version of his name, James, like Maryam's son. Johanan is the youngest, maybe fifteen with shoulder-length black hair, penetrating brown eyes, and wisps of a beard. The others smile and make a little bow to her. Johanan looks her straight in the eye and she feels like she should know him—perhaps she's seen him somewhere before. There is also another with a Greek name of Philip, and his brother, Nathaniel.

They each politely greet Maryam and James. Maryam's James is quiet with a poorly-disguised scowl on his face. It is obvious he doesn't approve of his big brother having disciples. Maryam notices that Johanan ben Zebediah is still looking at her when the others have followed Jesus into the house where the feast is to be held.

There is quite a crowd and Maryam's daughter, Elisheva is at the head table with her husband, Abram. Little Maryam is not to be seen. She is with her husband in the *chuppah* room and they will come out when they are ready. Some younger people that Maryam doesn't recognize are standing around the door of one of the rooms off the inner courtyard of the house, talking to each other and laughing.

Someone surprises her by addressing her. "I am very glad to meet you. He has spoken of you many times."

Maryam turns and realizes that Johanan has not left her side, though James and the family have. And it is he that has spoken to her. He is young, she thinks, but good-hearted, and considerate. There is a kindness in his eyes that Maryam likes.

"How do you know my son?" she asks.

"We were followers of Johanan the baptizer and with him in the desert."

"That is my cousin's son!" Maryam blurts out in surprise.

Johanan's eyes open wider. "Really? He is a holy man. He told us to follow this Jesus of Nazareth, your son. We have seen much in just a few weeks."

"But who are you all? Certainly you have not spent your lives in the desert."

"No. Philip and Andraus and I were with Johanan the baptizer. We are mostly fishermen from Capernaum. But we are looking for the salvation of Israel, and we heard of Johanan in the desert. When we found your son, we went and got our brothers."

A loud group shout interrupts Maryam and Johanan. The young people gathered around the room doors are waving their arms and cheering in approval. Little Maryam comes out smiling and blushing, holding the hand of a young man, who waves a bloody cloth in the air. Maryam can see from her granddaughter's eyes that she is happy and that she loves the young man. That is good. Such a thing is too rare. Let them love each other the way she loved Joseph.

MEDITATION NINE: THE STORM ARRIVES

People are moving to the tables as the food is brought out by hired servants. Maryam gasps silently at the costliness of everything she is seeing, many baskets of food and at least five servants. She hopes the family has not gone into debt to some Romanized over-lord for this feast. Elisheva comes and takes her by the hand.

"Mother, you are to sit at the high table beside me, as grandmother of the bride."

Once seated, Maryam talks a little with her daughter, but there isn't much news. Elisheva and Abram are paying for most of this, but his trade is thriving, so they can handle it. Elisheva is happy. The other daughters will soon be grown and married. Sunrise, sunset.

First chance she gets, Maryam gets up and wanders over to her family table, where her folks are as well, and Jesus and his followers. She sits by Jesus, who is leaning back on the bench and not engaged in conversation. She leans close to him and simply says,

"Tell me."

"I am announcing the coming of the Kingdom of God, Mother."

A chill runs through her, or is it a thrill? "Tell me," she repeats.

He tells her of the months passed, of where he's gone and how crowds are forming to hear him. She is about to comment when she notices the father of the groom and Abram in heated conversation at the head table. She gets up and goes over. They are arguing about the fact that it's only late in the first day and they are out of wine. Maryam's mind goes back to her own wedding with Joseph and her father's anguish and shame at having failed to provide.

She sets her face. No. Not again. I will not allow it. She walks back to Jesus, who is sitting with Johanan now. She looks down at him and he turns and looks up to her.

"They have no more wine."

He looks at her and says, "What does that have to do with me? My hour is not yet come."

Many translations have something more along the lines of 'Woman, what have I to do with you?' which sounds pretty rude. But the Greek is more like "this ain't my problem." And this is another pivotal moment. Catholic teaching holds that this moment shows us how Mary can move the heart of God. I would agree. But though I think she is powerful this way, given her son's parable of the unjust judge,[1] all of us have to some

---

1. Luke 18:1-8

degree this power because God grants it. To put it simply, God has invited us to nag him. Maryam is not afraid to do that. And when people even today ask for her prayers—not pray to her as a goddess—she has a history of nagging her son on our behalf.

She looks at him fixedly. She is his mother. She turns without a word and goes to the head-servant. "See that man sitting at the table over there?" she says, pointing out Jesus, who is looking at her.

"Yes, ma'am."

"He has a solution to the wine problem. Do whatever he tells you."

The servant looks perplexed but Maryam stares him down. After a moment he lets out a breath and walks up to Jesus. Jesus rises and they go off to the back of the house, with Johanan following in curiosity. After about maybe a quarter hour, the servants come in bearing a large pot normally used for ritual cleansing. Jesus has returned to his seat, but Johanan is standing behind the servants with the pot. Maryam goes over to join him. Abram, her son-in-law, comes over just as Maryam comes up and dips his cup in the pot, drawing out the liquid. He drinks and his eyes grow big.

"This is better than the first wine! You've held the best for last!"

The servant takes the jar around and starts replenishing everyone's cup.

Maryam grabs Johanan's arm and asks in a low voice. "What did my son do?"

"He told them to fill the jars with water and take it to that man. That's all."

Maryam smiles, walks over to where Jesus is sitting, sits down next to him and kisses him on the cheek. Again I want to emphasize that the role that Catholics claim for Maryam is no different than the role that we can all play. And as we grow closer to God, our prayers become more selfless and right, and our answers more certain. Maryam was and is close to her son. The Catholic and Orthodox belief is not that Mary is some favored goddess, but that we can ask this woman close to Christ to pray for us via the medium of the Holy Spirit, just as we can ask the woman at our church whom we respect for her faith to pray for us. My mentor, C.S. Lewis writes:

> Can we believe that God ever really modifies His action in response to the suggestions of men? For infinite wisdom does not need telling what is best, and infinite goodness needs no urging to do it. But neither does God need any of those things that are done by finite agents, whether living or inanimate. He could, if He chose,

MEDITATION NINE: THE STORM ARRIVES

repair our bodies miraculously without food; or give us food without the aid of farmers, bakers, and butchers; or knowledge without the aid of learned men; or convert the heathen without missionaries. Instead, He allows soils and weather and animals and the muscles, minds, and wills of men to co-operate in the execution of His will. "God," said Pascal, "instituted prayer in order to lend to His creatures the dignity of causality." But not only prayer; whenever we act at all He lends us that dignity. It is not really stranger, nor less strange, that my prayers should affect the course of events than that my other actions should do so. They have not advised or changed God's mind—that is, His over-all purpose.[2]

And yet, there is one more thing about this event that is often overlooked. The Gospel of John tells us that this miracle of making water into wine in Cana was the first miracle Jesus did.[3] What may escape the notice of some of is that he *did it at his mother's urging*. Think about that for a few minutes. And then consider all the other miracles. The other miracles generally fall out that someone asks Jesus for help. It's either that or the crowds pressing around him around are hungry. As Lewis quotes Pascal: "God instituted prayer in order to lend to His creatures the dignity of causality."

God waits to be asked.

After three days Maryam is riding her donkey south, being led by her James and thinking about all the events that had passed. Little Zechariah and Elisha, her grandsons by James, are riding in front of her on the donkey's withers, as the journey has been too much for them. She holds them tight to her. There is the slow clip-clop of hooves and the low talking of the family walking all around her. Her mind is on the last sight of Jesus walking the opposite direction with his six followers. Her heart has gone with him.

It is a half year or more before she sees him again, and this time, there is no peace. She is bombarded almost daily with gossip about him: he preaches in synagogues everywhere and with authority; he threw all the merchants out of the Temple in Jerusalem and started a riot. But what makes Maryam's heart stir is that time and again, people tell her that he has healed the sick and the lepers. So imagine Maryam's shock and surprise one Shabat day when she is going with James and Ana and the boys to the synagogue as they do every week, and she sees her Jesus across the room with a group of strange men, no doubt his followers, around him. She recognizes a few, especially that nice Johanan ben Zebediah, who sees

---

2. Lewis, "The Efficacy of Prayer", 3-4.
3. John 2:11

her and smiles. The leader of the village synagogue steps over to her Jesus, whom this man has known from boyhood. He whispers something to Jesus, who steps up, covering his head in his cloak, and takes the Torah scroll, here in this synagogue where he first read as a man some twenty years ago. Maryam is almost unable to breath, her suspense is so powerful. The scroll of the prophet Isaiah is handed to Jesus. Unrolling it, he finds a passage and reads aloud:

> The Spirit of the Lord is on me,
> because he has anointed me
> to proclaim good news to the poor.
> He has sent me to proclaim freedom for the prisoners
> and recovery of sight for the blind,
> to set the oppressed free,
> to proclaim the year of the Lord's favor.

Then Jesus rolls up the scroll, gives it back to the attendant and sits down. The room is dead silent and riveted on the next word of this local boy they've heard so much about

Her son says "Today this scripture is fulfilled in your hearing." He then launches into a talk about the arrival of the Kingdom of God. Her heart soars to hear it, but it doesn't last. Maryam hears the disharmony, like a crack forming in a perfect pot.

"Isn't this Joseph's son?" old Levi the tailor whispers.

"We know his brothers and sisters!" Elihu the baker answers too loudly.

Jesus hears them and stops. "Surely you will quote this proverb to me: 'Physician, heal yourself!' And you will tell me, 'Do here in your hometown what we have heard that you did in Capernaum.'"

There is a hubbub of voices at this. It is true that since his arrival, Jesus hasn't performed any of the miracles that they've heard of. But then they haven't asked him to. After all, he's just a local boy. Maryam knows her son too well. She knows that he won't spare his old friends and neighbors what he really thinks. He's too much like his mother this way. Jesus interrupts them.

"Truly I tell you, no prophet is accepted in his hometown. I assure you that there were many widows in Israel in Elijah's time, when the sky was shut for three and a half years and there was a severe famine throughout the land. Yet Elijah was not sent to any of them, but to a widow in

Zarephath in the region of Sidon. And there were many in Israel with leprosy in the time of Elisha the prophet, yet not one of them was cleansed—only Naaman the Syrian."

As he's saying this not-very-complimentary review of history, Maryam, even from where the women sit, on the outer periphery, behind the woven screen, can feel the room tense and then grow in rage. Is this upstart carpenter's boy suggesting that we're not really Yahweh's people? Whispering turns to muttering, which turns to shouting. Voices grow louder from the men till everyone is shouting and no one can hear Jesus. Jesus and his followers get up and leave the synagogue and the crowd of men surges after him to the far end of town, where Maryam knows there is a cliff. The infuriated men grab Jesus and push him toward the cliff. She runs after the mob of her friends and neighbors who have all turned into howling animals. Terror grips her heart and she dashes after them. My son! My son! My son!

She herself is crying "No! No!" but no one hears her over the men shouting. The followers and her sons, James, and Joseph and Judah and Shimon, try to intervene, but are pushed away. Maryam fights her way forward to the back of the mob. At the edge of the cliff, her Jesus turns and looks them all in the eye the way he once looked a Roman soldier in the eye. One by one the mob strangely falls silent as Jesus looks each one individually. One by one, they look down in shame and embarrassment at their hands. Some had picked up stones. They now drop them. Jesus says nothing, but quietly moves through the crowd and down the road to Sepphoris. His followers run and catch up with him. Maryam watches him go. She wipes the tears from her face.

"Mama, come home," Ana says, gently pulling her arm.

Meditation Ten: Desperate Measures

A WHILE BACK I defined holiness, this thing that Mary was given as a grace, in terms of Jesus' own definition. Protestants, some of them, might have a bit of a problem with this. In Protestantism there is a certain sensitivity to Pelagianism, that is believing that you can, by your good works, earn your way to Heaven and impress God. Protestants reject this and Rome and the Orthodox do as well, but back in the 1500s Protestants believed that Rome and fallen back into Pelagianism, a large part of the reason for the Reformation. And I can hear some Protestants now looking at my definition and saying, "this is Pelagianism."

No, not really.

If I looked at that list of things that Jesus taught us, and said to myself something like, "Ok, I'm going to do all these things, and golly, God is going to be impressed." Yes, that would be Pelagianism. It would also be a recipe for failure. If, on the other hand, knowing myself a screw-up, unsteady, self-indulgent, in short, a sinner, I look at the standard Jesus has set, and depending on the grace of God, try and move toward that holiness, God will support that effort. And that is what he wants of us. That is why I think this is the obvious definition that we like to ignore or replace. Why? Well, for one thing, it's awful damn tough to do. Only with God's grace is it even remotely possible.

Love my enemies?
When someone robs me, give them more?
Do good to those who hate me?
Give to whomever asks?
You've got to be kidding. No way.
But God says "Yes way."

We really don't have a choice. Holiness is a pretty tough road and doesn't sound like much fun. But I find that when I trust God, on the all too rare occasions that I do, things work out in remarkable and unexpected ways.

And I believe that was Mary's experience. She dived head first into trust, from the moment Gabriel gave her a choice, and she never looked back. Mary full of grace; and she was.

What's really remarkable is that we all have that same opportunity. Some of us grasp it with both hands, like Francis of Assisi. Most of us prefer the Religion of Luck, keeping God like a divine fire extinguisher, at arm's length, just in case we need him if our precious luck runs out. I think for the Israelites in the Old Testament, this was the appeal of idols. Idols were manageable gods who didn't much interfere with daily life and could be appealed to when the luck ran thin. Yahweh was a jealous god who demanded one's heart, mind, and soul. And he was even so unreasonable as to demand we love our neighbor as ourselves.

Most of us treat God as if he were an idol.

And this is why I'm going to go even further out on a limb here; I think, not long after this alarming homecoming, Maryam left home and started following her son around the countryside. Maryam became a disciple. In the movie, *Mary of Nazareth*, she does exactly that, which is part of the reason I like the movie in spite of the pretty, Caucasian Mary. In the movie, she goes to see Jesus with an uncle—interesting how this Catholic version dumps even the cousins in its effort to evade the possibility of brothers—to rein in Jesus. And Jesus says his line about my mother and brothers are those who do the will of God. The uncle walks away disgusted. Mary stays with her son. This makes sense to me. Otherwise, we have to explain why she hopped a flight to be at the crucifixion but wasn't hanging around before that. If she was at the crucifixion, at some point, she left home to be with Jesus in his rambles. My guess is that it happened sooner than later. And we know that she came with Jesus' brothers not long after the fiasco at the Nazareth synagogue.

Since the Gospels aren't dated, and we have repetitions of certain events across them, scholars over the years have constructed something called a "harmony of the Gospels", which is a rough timeline that attempts to coordinate the events told in the Gospels in a reasonable chronological order. We can't be sure these are correct, and there are several versions, but if we hold that the Gospels are more or less chronological in their telling, we can deduce that somewhere not long after this disastrous home visit, Jesus gets a visit from his brothers and Maryam. So we know that she and the brothers went to rein in Jesus. Either, as in the movie, she stayed, or she went back around the time of the arrest and crucifixion. For a woman to make a journey of that distance alone is not something that was done. It was dangerous enough for men. At least, if she came with the brothers and then stayed, we know she made the journey. I am, of course, guessing based on the most logical possibilities, but this one is a coin flip, as was the brothers issue. For the purposes of this , I'm going to agree with the *Mary of Nazareth* movie and conclude that she stayed with Jesus at this point and joined the group of women that followed Jesus around.

It would have started with James being worked up at the recent blow-out at the synagogue. James calls a meeting of his siblings.

"This has got to stop!" he yells, waving his arms.

Ana and Elisheva are there. Dvorah just gave birth to her fifth child and is recovering at home after a frighteningly difficult birth that almost took her life. Joseph and Judah have taken the day off from farming to attend and agree whole-heartedly with James. The girls say little.

Ana says, "You have never understood him, James."

"What does that matter! He's acting like a madman. He'll get himself killed. We have to bring him home and keep him quiet. The Romans will go after him, mark my words."

"Quite right," says Judah, and Joseph agrees.

All through this, Maryam has sat listening, pained to her heart, the sword piercing it again. She knows that she cannot stop James and she knows that Ana is right. She wonders if she should use her authority to squash this, but it is not in her nature to bind people. And James' idea of going to see Jesus has excited her. If James goes, she can go. She knows that she has been contemplating the irresponsible and going by herself. All these emotions swirl around her.

Shimon speaks up, "You're wrong, James."

Shimon was always closer to Jesus than any of the other brothers—eldest and youngest. His wife's father had only one daughter and no sons. So he has brought Shimon into the weaving and dying business, creating fine and colorful clothing for the wealthy and those who played nice with the Romans. "You don't understand Jesus" Shimon adds. "And I'm not going to have any part of this."

James glares at him, but Shimon doesn't seem to care. He goes up to Maryam and opens the bag he'd brought. "I've made a cloak for Jesus. Can you give this to him?" He pulls out a fine, deep red woven cloak, something that wealthy men might wear. I know this seems a reach, but how else did Jesus get such a fine cloak that the Roman soldiers crucifying

MEDITATION TEN: DESPERATE MEASURES

him drew lots for it rather than chop it up? Shimon digs deeper into the bag and pulls out a second cloak, a rich blue one. "And Mother, this is for you." Ok, ok, I know I said Maryam never wore dyed clothes, but having a connection like this might have made an exception. And besides, I like Maryam in blue as much as anyone.

Shimon gives James an angry look and walks out of the house. James snorts and goes about making the preparations. Maryam finally speaks. Here she will impose what authority she has.

"I am going with you, son."

"Mother, there is no need. We will make him see sense and bring him home . . . ."

"I'm not asking you James. I am going with you."

He stops what he's doing, arrested by the firmness of her tone. He knows his mother well enough to know when she has set her face, there is no changing her mind.

"Very well, Mother."

A few days later, Maryam is riding the donkey again, with James, Joseph, and Judah leading her. She is happier than she has been for a long time. Every mile closer to seeing Jesus makes her feel excited in a way that surprises her. It is possible to miss someone and not feel how deeply they leave a hole in your heart until something starts to change? They don't have to go far. Jesus has set up in a house at Capernaum, and James has heard that he's there. The road goes north through Sepphoris again. Maryam finds riding through the splendid Roman city brings her to tears. Somewhere in this shining mass of brass and stone, there is a wall that had to be rebuilt after it fell on her Joseph. She feels his presence somehow in this place, and though she loves to think of him, she is relieved when the grand avenues and stone palaces fall behind them.

They turn east at the junction, instead of north to Cana, where her granddaughter lives, and as the sun goes down, they come out of a long valley and down a hillside to the seaside village of Magdala, splayed on the western shore with its small houses and its fishing boats tied up on the beach. Laying before them, silver and purple in the dying light, is the Sea of Galilee. Maryam remembers seeing the southern shore on the few trips they were able to make to Jerusalem, but now she sees it spread out before her like a giant platter from horizon to horizon, with a little strip of shore across the way in sepia brown. They find an inn and spend the night wrapped in blankets on a series of straw mats in a small back room. It's not very comfortable, but just being this much closer to Jesus makes Maryam so happy in a quiet way, that she falls asleep easily.

They are off at first light after a piece of bread. Maryam feels almost giddy. They pass through Gennesaret by mid-morning, with the broad blue of the sea to their right, the small waves lapping endlessly, and the fishing boats like small dots far out into the middle of the sea. The air smells good, the smell of a large body of water. Maryam understands why Jesus chose this place to live, besides the fact that nobody in Nazareth believes in him, except Shimon, Ana, Dvorah, and of course, herself. She wonders what Joseph would have thought of this turn of events. Joseph knew and she knew, that Jesus was born very special, and not Joseph's son. None of the others in the family know, though Dvorah used to ask pointed questions about her big brother. She sensed something. Maryam wishes that James could sense it too, and young Joseph and Judah. But she cannot force her sons to understand.

The town of Capernaum appears ahead to the north. Maryam can feel her heart beating. It looks like any other Galilean town till they get close. People are everywhere. The small town is overwhelmed with visitors. Maryam only remembers seeing this many people in one place when they were in Jerusalem. Today, in our era of open-air concerts, we can easily picture such a crowd. It was totally strange to Maryam and her sons. Maryam can see James sag a little as they go along. She knows he is just now realizing that what he has come to do is beyond him. Still they press on. A bystander directs them to the house where Jesus and his followers stay. There is a mob gathered around the small house, not unlike Maryam's own house. They all talk and the quiet of the village is broken by the buzz of many voices. Maryam stops James and dismounts. They press into the crowd as far as they can go, but are still ten feet or more from the door in the press of people. James may be a bit daunted, but he still has his own share of setting his face. He says loudly, "Let us pass. We are the mother and brothers of Jesus. Let us pass. We are the mother and brothers of Jesus."

People turn and look at them, and then press to one side or the other. James takes Maryam's hand, while Judah and Joseph follow, and they thread their way through the masses to the door, where the crowd is even thicker. They have to stop. James repeats his call, but no one can move. Instead people start passing the message forward across the crowded dirt courtyard. Maryam can see her Jesus talking to people maybe twenty yards away over a sea of heads. The message is passed up.

MEDITATION TEN: DESPERATE MEASURES

Jesus looks up, sees them, and says loudly "My mother and my brothers are those who hear the word of God and carry it out."

Maryam can hear James sputter helplessly. He turns, pulling her hand. "Come on. It's no use." Both he and her other sons turn to go.

She pulls her hand free of his. "I'm staying."

"Mother, this is madness. Not you too."

"I'm staying, son."

"Mother . . . "

"I'm staying, son."

Anger crosses his brow and he storms off, explaining as he leaves to Judah and Joseph, who keep looking back as if she will still come with them.

Maryam turns back and locks eyes with Jesus. Whatever James heard, Maryam heard a choice. But she made that choice long ago, in a lonely room speaking to an archangel. A man next to her shouts, "Let her pass! It is his mother!" The crowd presses with difficulty to one side or the other and people offer their hands as she squeezes forward, person by person, pressing uncomfortably close to each one. Finally, after the longest time, she finds herself in the inmost circle and there is that nice Johanan ben Zebediah handing her past him. Jesus is there. She doesn't even wait, but throws herself in his arms with hundreds of people looking on. She doesn't care. Let them look.

There is an approving murmur in the crowd, in this era before hand applause, a later, Roman invention, and some feet are stomped in approval. After a long embrace, Maryam steps back down to where Johanan is. He guides her over to a group of eleven women, and Maryam soon learns that her Jesus has women disciples as well. When Johanan introduces her at Jesus's mother, they all open their arms to her and embrace her, calling her "Mother." Maryam has just gained eleven more daughters. Two of the women are well-dressed, Joanna, and Susanna. The rest are plainly and poorly dressed like herself, save for her blue cloak. There are even two other Maryams: surprisingly, one is her sister-in-law, the wife of Joseph's deceased brother, Cleopas, and another younger woman from Magdala. Maryam is much taken with this girl from Magdala. She is dark-haired, and thin, as if she had almost died of hunger or disease and was recovering. Perhaps this was so. Her brown eyes were both gaunt and yet beautiful for the kindness and the sadness that radiated from them. And when Jesus began to speak again and all fell quiet, it was the girl from Magdala who leaned forward and watched him with all the longing of spirit that could be expressed.

Jesus begins to speak again, and the message is the one we would associate with the Sermon on the Mount. If there are different versions of this, I think it can be chalked up to Jesus having something of what a politician today would call a "stump speech," that might vary a bit from time to time, but was basically consistent. Politicians do this to put out a consistent message over time and across various locations. For like them, Jesus can't know which of his hearers have heard him before and to which his message of the Kingdom of God is fresh, so he is forced to a certain amount of repetition.

For Maryam it comes like a symphony: all the things she hoped for when this baby came upon her in such a miraculous way have come to fruition. Over the next few months, she will hear this again and again and never tire of it. *Adonai* has not failed her. Her heart is soaring. She hopes that people will listen, and change and that somehow this nightmare of a Roman occupation will be overcome by this new and holier Israel. And considering that Luke's Gospel is based on Mark, with many additions, and that Luke most likely interviewed Mary, isn't it just possible that the extra source Luke had was Mary herself, who followed her son around Palestine for the better part of two years. Thus the Gospel of Luke, in many respects, is the Gospel of Mary.

She also finds herself more and more drawn to this girl from Magdala that shares her name. Maryam simply calls her "*barta*", the Aramaic word for daughter, and the two form a bond. And so Maryam becomes the matriarch a second time, this time to a band of women, varying in size, that walk the dusty roads and follow Jesus for the next two years. At times, Jesus does go off with his twelve closest disciples. But just as often the band of men and women is together. With the help of the wealthier women, these ladies provide for Jesus and his disciples.

Maryam listens to her son's preaching, more and more thrilled and confirmed in the sense that she has that the difficult thing she was given to do has come to flower, and that all will be well in the future. Her optimism soars. Six months into her long wander after Jesus up and down between Judah and Galilee, her heart soars even higher. Her daughter, Ana, appears at the house in Capernaum one day, refusing to be any longer parted from her mother. Shimon has brought her, and he spends some close time with his big brother, Jesus, before he returns to Nazareth. And the daughters of Maryam, of blood and of heart, follow Jesus joyfully around the countryside, wearing out their sandals but warming their hearts.

Meditation Eleven: The Very Worst That Could Possibly Happen

IT'S THE INCREASINGLY TERSE exchanges with the Pharisees in Judea that give Maryam her first sense of foreboding. We don't usually think of this. For most of us, we think of Mary showing up right at the crucifixion and this doesn't seem odd to us. But then we live in a world where things move quickly, where if I knew my cousin in Maine was predicted to live no more than a week, though I live in California, I could be on a plane in the next few hours and be there, 3,000 miles away. The idea of Mary suddenly showing up at the cross doesn't surprise us. In our world, people do just show up.

But not in the first century.

This is why I have had Mary following Jesus around since the mother-and-brothers incident. It was a three day journey from Galilee to Jerusalem in those days on foot, maybe two if you were athletic and pushed the pace. Today, Google maps tells me that I can make the journey in an hour and 58 minutes by car, using mainly Route 6. So for Mary to have been present at the crucifixion, she was with Jesus before it, most likely having come down from Galilee when he did. Women in the first century didn't just hop a plane. They didn't even travel alone. Some man had to bring Mary to Jesus.

And that means that Mary had her own *via dolorosa*. She was there for the whole agonizing show. And this would have been the worst of the swords that Simeon predicted. Our four Gospel accounts are problematic. The focus is on Jesus and the Twelve, and sometimes only on Peter, James, and John. And every once in a while, we get a aside on the women, who followed them everywhere.[1] The focus on the Twelve is symbolic, as in the twelve tribes of Israel, but we know there were more dedicated male disciples than that. In Acts 1 we read of Peter speaking to all the followers of Jesus about replacing Judas, so that the inner ring is once again the symbolic twelve:

1. Luke 8:1-3

> 21 So one of the men who have accompanied us during all the time the Lord Jesus went in and out among us, 22 beginning from the baptism of John until the day when he was taken up from us—one of these must become a witness with us to his resurrection."
>
> 23 So they proposed two, Joseph called Barsabbas who was also known as Justus, and Matthias. (NRSV)

They draw lots and Matthias becomes one of the Twelve. What's clear from this is that there are at least two others beside the Twelve that have been close to Jesus from day one, and I can't believe there are only two. At one point there are 72[2], though there seems to have been some drop-off when Jesus calls himself the Bread of Life.[3] Yet, the Gospel writers write pretty consistently about "the Twelve". The others aren't even mentioned. They are assumed. I believe it was the same with the women.

We have only scattered references to the women, as if they dropped in every once in a while. That, of course, is just as ridiculous as the idea of Mary hopping a flight from Nazareth when John texts her that Jesus has been arrested. After the Resurrection, the disciples meet around Mary.[4] Though we only hear about the Twelve in the Garden of Gethsemane and at the Last Supper, it's the women who show up at the crucifixion, with John, who of the Twelve, is the only one to recover from the shame of Gethsemane and risk his life to stand by the cross of Jesus. Feminist scholars would tell is that the writers of the New Testament accounts are so patriarchal that the ever-present women are only mentioned when necessary, being a part of the background like the table, the chairs, and the windows. I suspect there is a lot of truth to this. Where were the women who followed everywhere at the final Passover? You mean that Christ's mother was at the crucifixion a few hours later but not invited to the Passover with her son? Maybe her plane hadn't landed at Ben Gurion airport yet. The thought is ridiculous. And we're told that the women provided for Jesus and the disciples for years. Traditionally, women prepared food. And the Last Supper, this final Passover was for some strange reason prepared by men, with the women told to go off somewhere else? The Passover, after all, was a family ceremony traditionally celebrated by the men and the women together.

I think it far more likely that the women, including Mary, prepared the meal and sat off toward the perimeter, living up to the code of the time

2. Luke 10
3. John 6:61-66
4. Acts 1:14

MEDITATION ELEVEN: THE VERY WORST THAT COULD POSSIBLY HAPPEN

that made women separate from men in anything of importance. Dan Brown's fantasy has Mary Magdalene as the figure sitting next to Jesus in DaVinci's painting of the Last Supper. I'm not sure she was sitting right next to Jesus, but I believe she, and Mary the Mother of Christ and all the women were seated somewhere in the room. If not, where did the women have Passover? Gender-segregated Passovers were unknown to the Jews. Or is it just that the Gospel writers were focused in on the prime actors, and left the minor actors out.

One of C.S. Lewis' arguments for the authenticity of the Gospels is how badly, by modern standards, they were written. To leave out major characters like Mary, mother of Christ, our Maryam, and Mary Magdalene, our Magdala, is bad narrative technique. The Gospel writers knew nothing of writing technique. Except for John, they seem to be mainly focused in the accounts of that night on the institution of the Eucharist and the accusation and the denials of betrayal. After that's out of the way, these writers move the scene swiftly to the garden where the betrayal is to take place. The women, sitting quietly at the meal, were not important enough for the Gospel writers to mention, at least in those writers' minds.

But before I move on, I want to point out the thing that frustrates so many people right and left. Feminists are glad to see that Jesus had women in his following, but aggrieved that the Twelve is all male. Social conservatives tend to cover over or minimize the presence of women at all, as if they flew in and out of Jesus life for specific scenes, such as the Resurrection, they way movie directors move actors off and on camera.

I would say that Jesus was revolutionary in that he included women in the heart of his movement. But like St Paul later, he did not feel the need to attack cultural norms so much as try to get people to open their hearts to the Kingdom of God. So Jesus freed no slaves, nor appointed any women to leadership. But women were constantly and centrally involved in his ministry. Our realizations that slavery was evil and that women are equally valid and competent human beings have come slowly over the centuries and in the face of rooted cultural values, but those realizations have been true and moral. I do wonder what the effect would have been had Our Lord attacked these matters while here. When you think about it, Jesus didn't really heal all the people in Israel who were sick, but only the few that came to him. His efforts on earth did not encompass sweeping social change, or some sort of universal repair of all wrongs, so much as just launching the Kingdom. But then, Jesus seems to have been carrying out something like a three-year commando raid on evil; I imagine his raid didn't have the time to liberate all captives. That last part falls to us as the Body of Christ, and what we don't finish is left to the Second Coming.

So Maryam is in the room at the table, with her daughters, the one biological and the rest of her heart, when her Jesus tells them all amazing things that Johanan later wrote down. Then Jesus, having finished a remarkable new take on the bread and the wine, reveals that he is about to be betrayed. Her heart sinks. No, *Adonai* could not let this happen to his own son. The shouting and the consternation is shared by the women as well. Then Judas goes out. No one gets it. They think he's running yet another errand. My guess? Maryam knew. She knew the fix was in on Judas. Why do I think that? Because in my experience, women read people better than men do. So when Judas leaves the room, Maryam feels a chill of terror go through her and shivers. No, no, no. It's not supposed to go down this way. Maryam feels like the earth is caving in under her at the edge of a cliff and she can't do anything to stop it. She remembers vividly that horrible day in Nazareth when her neighbors almost killed her son.

But her Jesus changes the tone and says incredible things. He is the Way to *Adonai*. He will send the Spirit of *Adonai* to them. He is the vine and they are the branches. The Spirit will guide them. In his Father's house there are many homes for them. Their grief will turn to joy.

Grief? Maryam's heart trembles.

But after the high of those words, the night gets worse. The women remain in the hired room while Jesus takes the Twelve and a few other men out to Gethsemane. Then hours later, Johanan rushes in, dirty, with tear stains on his cheeks. His cloak is mud-spattered. He wakes them with a shout.

"They've arrested Jesus!" he gasps between sucking in breaths. There is a second pause of silence which seems to last a millennium. Then there is no waiting. They question Johanan closely and he tells them of everything in the garden, even the prayers for a change of fate from Jesus and his blood sweat. Maryam bundles up in an extra cloak and the other women follow her lead. There is one advantage in this patriarchal culture to being a woman: you can go almost anywhere and be invisible if you keep your mouth shut. Just as the woman were invisible for large stretches to the writers of the Gospels, so they can be invisible to guards and gatekeepers.

"Let us go to Jesus," Maryam states firmly and the other women nod. They leave the room in a whoosh of cloaks through the door. They march through the darkened streets of Jerusalem with Johanan in tow. Within half an hour, they find themselves at a gate to the home of Caiphas, the High Priest. The guards let them pass without a word, though strangely, just as they're coming in, Petros of their group goes plunging out the gate and into the dark without so much as a word to them. There is a fire there in the broad outer courtyard and some servants and extra guards standing around it. Through a second guarded gate, Maryam can see into the inner courtyard and the house with all the windows lit and angry voices shouting out into the chill night air.

Maryam and the women and Johanan settle around the fire and listen. The servants talk about Petros, who just rushed out. They are sure he was with Jesus. They should have had him arrested. Maryam sees fear in the eyes of the women around her but she does not move a muscle in her face. Let them think what they will and arrest whomever they want. She's not leaving Jesus. The others say nothing, but seeing the firmness in Maryam's face, they all seem to calm down. The servants who were talking of arrest all go off to work and things become quiet. The guards standing near them rotate to posts, and the other guards go off somewhere else, perhaps to sleep.

Johanan and the women stand around the fire by themselves. Some of the women sit by the fire back-to-back and sleep sitting up. Maryam stands and listens through the night. She thinks she should have seen this coming. There was the time a year or more ago when they got news that her fine young nephew, Johanan, Zechariah's and Elisheva's son, had been slaughtered by Herod. Johanan's disciples brought word that they have recovered most of the body and buried it. Then they fell in with Jesus' other followers. Maryam's heart was grieved then for senseless death of that beautiful little boy, whom she saw born.

What if *Adonai* lets Jesus die?

No. It couldn't be. No even possible, Why would there be all the miraculous events, the conception, the birth, the shepherds, the Persian astrologers, and Jesus' incredible miracles since and the way that his words open hearts? It just couldn't be. But her faith senses no strong reassurance. *Adonai* does unpredictable things. He always has. These thoughts are troubling her when there is a rush of voices and people in the next courtyard. Maryam, the women, and Johanan dash over to the gate to the inner courtyard, but are blocked by guards. A large armed party of Temple guards, in armor, with shields and spears, goes out and Jesus is in their midst, wrists bound, looking exhausted with dark rings under his eyes. His eyes for a moment meet hers and then he disappears out the far gate to the street on the other side with his guards. A train of weary old men, the Sanhedrin, stumble out the front door of the house behind the escort. Maryam recognizes one gray-bearded old man, in scarlet robes, Joseph of Arimithea, who has been with their group and Jesus for some of the time. She cries out his name. He sees her and comes over to the gate where guards are blocking the women. They let Joseph pass out to the women and he stops to talk with them.

"I am so sorry, Maryam. I tried to speak on his behalf, but your son has made bad enemies amongst the elders. They have condemned him to death for blasphemy and sent him to the Governor."

"Blasphemy?" Maryam retorts, her anger flaring. "What blasphemy?"

Joseph sighs, "He admitted that he was the Son of Yahweh."

Maryam opens her mouth to speak, but she of all people on Earth knows how true that statement is.

"I am so sorry," Joseph continues. "I will stay awake and see how things develop. With any luck, Pilate will think their charges foolish and set Jesus free. And then he *must, must* stay away from Jerusalem. But you are all exhausted. There is nothing to be done now. The Romans will keep him till morning. Pilate will see him when he's ready. He will not hurry to please the Sanhedrin. Come to my house and rest and take some food. Please, please."

Maryam lets herself be persuaded and the group goes to Joseph's large and fine home to sleep and eat. Maryam, in spite of her spinning mind, dozes off for several hours and is wakened only at midday by Johanan. The women wake up those sleeping and prepare to go. Joseph comes out to them with his servants, bearing fresh bread.

"Eat before you go. This day will be long no matter what. I will remain here and wait for news that will come my way. I will send to you if I find out something. But if you learn something, please send word to me. Where will you be?"

Johanan says through a mouthful of bread, "We will be outside Herod's Palace, where the Governor will hold court."

They finish the bread quickly. Maryam squeezes old Joseph's hand and whispers her gratitude. Then they are off through the streets, striding at a rapid pace. When they arrive at that ocher-colored walls and towers of Herod's Palace they find that the Romans have let a group come in to the first courtyard. A crowd of maybe a hundred people, mostly young men, unemployed day-laborers and street vendors, is clustered around a stage on a high wall. Johanan melts into the crowd and comes back to the women a few minutes later. Pilate will make an appearance today, he tells them. It

MEDITATION ELEVEN: THE VERY WORST THAT COULD POSSIBLY HAPPEN

seems that all the useless young men in Jerusalem are here for the entertainment. And most of them have been drinking wine freely.

As the women and Johanan stand waiting, Maryam can feel searing pain in her mind, and she knows that somehow she is being allowed to share what her son is going through in some courtyard not far from here. The hub-bub of the mob makes it impossible to hear much but she can feel the agony coming from somewhere. No! No! Not her sweet baby boy! Her mind goes suddenly fuzzy. Her knees start to buckle and Maryam of Magdala and Ana catch her.

"What's the matter, mother?" Ana asks urgently.

"They are torturing your brother," she whispers.

Ana does not seem to know how to reply, but she and Maryam of Magdala continue to hold up Maryam as the waves of pain flood her mind. Her sister-in-law, Maryam, wife of Cleopas, takes her hands and massages them. Joanna and Susana take turns supporting her. After a long while, it stops. Maryam is slowly more able to stand. They are there for hours. Johanan goes to find water-skins for them and more bread if he can get it. When he returns, they eat and drink and feel some strength returning. They are finishing when the buzz of conversation grows louder and something is happening on the stage high above them at the top of the wall. About five Roman soldiers fan out up there, and then the Governor appears, Pilate, in his fine white tunic and red Roman toga. He sits. More soldiers come out leading two prisoners, both of whom are bloody and beaten.

"Jesus!" Maryam cries, unable to help herself.

Shouts from the mob under the stage drown them out.

Pilate stands up and raises his hands. The courtyard slowly falls quiet. "Caesar is merciful and it is a custom that at the time of your Passover, I release a prisoner. Which one do you want me to release to you: Barabbas, or Jesus who is called your 'Messiah?'"

There is a buzzing in the crowd. Maryam doesn't hesitate. "Jesus!" she cries, "Jesus!" The women and Johanan take up her cry, but they are quickly drowned out by the mob crying "Barabbas!"

"Which of the two do you want me to release to you?" asks the governor.

"Barabbas!" the drunken young men roar.

"What shall I do, then, with Jesus who is called Messiah?" Pilate asks.

They mob roars again, "Crucify him!"

"Why? What crime has he committed?" asks Pilate.

But the mob howls, "Crucify him!"

Pilate stands looking at the mob, shaking his head. The Roman soldiers in the court lower their spears or draw their swords, waiting for an order to clear the courtyard or worse. Pilate beckons and a servant come out from the wings, carrying a basin. Pilate washes his hands in front of the crowd, drying them on a towel draped over the servant's arm. "I am innocent of this man's blood," he says. "It is your responsibility!" Then he strides off the stage in obvious disgust.

The mob shouts some unintelligible things in response to this, and then the show is over. Maryam's heart throbs as her battered Jesus is led out of sight.

"Where are they taking him?" she pleads.

Johanan says, "They will take him to Golgotha. If we hurry, there is a place on the streets nearby where he will have to pass us.

They rush through the crowd, Ana and Maryam of Magdala holding Maryam's hands and helping her to keep up. Eventually, they penetrate the narrow, winding maze of streets between white-washed walls and come to a wider boulevard where people are already stopped, forming clusters against the walls on each side. Johanan finds them a space and they plant themselves, looking up hill up the street.

"The Romans always come through here," he tells the women.

As they sit, Maryam realizes that her own mind is playing tricks on her. Time is slowing down and the voices of the crowd are dimming and getting far away and echoing. Today, we'd know that we were going into shock, but Maryam knows no such thing. So when the Roman soldiers push through and shove the crowd against the wall, she hardly hears. It seems far away. Then there is a dressed man carrying the cross, but it is not her Jesus. Yet, when she sees him directly behind, bloody, exhausted, a crown of cruel thorns shoved down over his brow, she comes away from the wall in one motion and her mind clears at the same time. Ana, Magdala, and Johanan catch her and hold her back, else she would have dared the Roman soldiers and gone to Jesus.

Jesus can barely walk, and his face is very bloody so he must hardly be able to see. He is stooped over, too weak to stand up. His hair is sweat-soaked and knotted. His mouth hangs open from exhaustion. Now he is no more than four feet away from them by modern measure. A buzz in the crowd sends the Roman guards to the opposite side of the narrow street, and much to everyone's surprise, his sister, Ana, lets go of Maryam and

MEDITATION ELEVEN: THE VERY WORST THAT COULD POSSIBLY HAPPEN

rushes to her brother's side, gently wiping his face with a fistful of her cloak. A Roman soldier steps up and shoves her back into Johanan's arms, with Jesus' blood on her cloak. The soldiers move on and Jesus staggers away till the column moves out of sight and the sightseers either break up or follow it. Johanan, Maryam, and the women follow the mob.

We have this moment in tradition as St Veronica wiping Jesus' face and coming away with a perfect face print. I'm not so sure about the face print, but "Veronica" is Latin for "true image." So it's more of a description of what she allegedly got for wiping Jesus' face than a name. We don't really know this woman's name. Plus, just blotting his face and thus getting some sort of image seems to me less likely and useful than wadding up a corner of one's cloak and cleaning the places that were bloody. So I have given this moment to his sister.

The train of prisoners and Jesus, surrounded by a dozen soldiers and a small mob makes its way out of the city gate and up to the round, bare, bleak hill appropriately named Golgotha, or "The Skull", where the Romans like to nail up their victims. Maryam forces herself to watch as they nail her baby boy to a wooden cross and hoist him up between two other prisoners. She feels her mind grow fuzzy again and Magdala, Ana, and Johanan have to support her. It grows dark and she loses track of time, not caring when a rain comes and drenches them. Her sons speaks occasionally in a raspy whisper, as he, like the others goes between the excruciating pain of standing on nails and the suffocating horror of hanging. She does not hear most of it, and tears blind her. The whole endless sequence has a nightmare quality to it, and she wonders if she's going to wake up. Please, please let her wake up. This cannot be happening. *Adonai* cannot fail her like this. Oh, my baby boy, my baby boy!

Then Jesus, in obvious agony, looks at her and her mind clears. Johanan is supporting her.

"Woman," he rasps out, "See your son. Son," he says directly to Johanan, "See your mother."

Now, this, of course, raises all kinds of questions. If Jesus had brothers, why this giving of his mother? Well, the question is equally valid if you go with the Catholic and Orthodox belief that the brothers and sisters mentioned in the Gospel were step-brothers and step-sisters, or even cousins. Why do this when Maryam had family? I cannot absolutely know, but I think this was one of the places that Our Lord was given s certain amount of foresight. I will explain later.

The fog of shock descends onto Maryam's mind. At some point her mind stirs from the dark waters in which she wades; they are taking down the body and they lay her bloody, cold, still baby boy in her arms for the last time. This is the moment of the *Pieta*. She remembers holding him, so tiny, in her arms in the stable at Bethlehem. Then Ana, and Magdala, and Johanan are leading her away. They find their way to the upper room again. Beyond exhausted, she sleeps.

When she wakes, it is midday. The room is full, not only of Johanan and the women, but Petros and the other Eleven now, plus the other male followers. They stay quiet and take turns watching the door. Nobody enters without being questioned. Maryam senses fear in them. But oddly, her mind, so foggy through the horror of yesterday, is now clear. She lays on her pallet between Ana and Magdala, watching the sunlight play through the window. What is this feeling in her heart? Strangely, she has a sense of well-being, as if somehow something good was coming. But her precious first son is dead. She can't explain it. Then something odd happens. She swears that she hears her Jesus laugh, like he did when he was a boy. The laugh lasts but a second, and quickly looking around she discerns that no one else heard it. Still, when grief should be crushing her heart, she feels so light. It is all strange.

After a long while, she rises and helps prepare food, from the leftovers. It is Shabat and the work to prepare food is kept to an absolute minimum. As they sit around the table in the far side of the room, Johanan quietly tells her that Joseph has come through for them. He let himself be ritually defiled and went in to see Pilate, respectfully asking for Jesus' body. Pilate granted it and Joseph has buried her son is his own fine tomb outside the city.

Magdala comments, "They did not properly put spices in his wrapping."

Ana says, "Tomorrow we will go and hope the tomb is still open so we can observe the proper rights for . . . . " She cannot finish, tears streaming down her face.

Shabat goes by quietly but also painfully. Still, Maryam senses something light and joyous just beyond the horizon. She cannot explain it.

Meditation Twelve: The Surprises of *Adonai*

MARYAM WAKES AT FIRST light on the morning of the third day. Women are bustling about, though quietly. It's Magdala, Joanna, her sister-in-law, Maryam of Cleopas, and another older Maryam who is the mother of one of the twelve, known as Salome. Ana, laying by her mother on a pallet in the corner, explains that she will stay in the room with Maryam, for they fear that the sight of her son's body would be too much for her. Ana does not know the medical definition of shock, but she knows that her mother was barely able to stay conscious through Friday's horrors. She is not anxious to expose her mother to more of it.

Maryam asks her, "Don't you want to go too?"

"No, Mama. I will stay here with you."

The door is barely opened, and the four women slip quietly out. The door closes fast behind them.

It is interesting in the accounts of the Gospel writers how they differently describe which women went to the tomb to find it empty on that first Easter morning. Luke's account is the fullest and he adds, ". . . the women who had come with him from Galilee followed and saw the tomb and how his body was laid."[1] Mark says much the same in 15:40,41. And Luke goes on with the fullest roll call of the women who became the first witnesses to the Resurrection. So in that verse we learn that the women had been with them all along, even if one could easily get the impression that Jesus went around with only the Twelve. This is further confirmation that the Gospel writers edit out the non-Twelve and the women except when the story line forces them to include these people.

But back to our Maryam, she feels strangely light, considering that she watched her son being tortured to death two days ago. Again, she hears the sound of Jesus' laugh, the laugh he had as a boy, and she looks around the room. Nobody else seems to notice. She must be hearing things.

---

1. Luke 23:55

There is a commotion at the door. Two men are trying to enter and they are being questioned by one of the Twelve watching the door. Then Johanan interrupts them and says, "This is the Lord's brothers. Let them in." In walk James and Shimon. They see their sister and their mother at once across the room and go to them. Maryam stands and joys in the embrace of her two strong sons. This may sound odd here, but we know from Acts 1:14 that the post-Resurrection followers gathered around Maryam and Jesus' brothers. Those brothers had to arrive sometime. And it wasn't after they got the text that Jesus had be executed by the Romans and then they hoped an El Al flight from Nazareth to Ben Gurion airport. Again, we think in modern terms where instant communication and rapid travel are readily available. If the brothers were there, they came at some point of their own volition. If they came as result of the death of Jesus, they would have taken at least a week to arrive, given the time it would take for someone to walk up to Nazareth, tell them, for them to prepare and to walk down to Jerusalem.

So James, Shimon, Ana, and our Maryam leave off hugging after a while and sit down in the corner for a family huddle. Ana recounts in detail the events of the last few weeks and hours. James tells his mother, with tears streaking down his cheeks,

"I am so sorry, Mother. I've been so blind. Shimon came and talked to me. He made me see. And now I'm too late."

"I don't know about that," Maryam says, though she's not really sure why she said it. And before they can react, Maryam drops a bomb on them. Only Joseph knew. "There is something I must tell you all about your brother. He was not the son of your father." Maryam sees the shock in here children's eyes. "Shortly before my marriage, I was visited by a messenger of *Adonai* who looked like fire. He told me I would bear *Adonai's* son. When I told your father, to whom I was betrothed at the time, he was preparing to cancel our marriage. But *Adonai* spoke to him in a dream. Your father knew that Jesus was special, that he belonged to *Adonai* and not to us. You, Ana and Shimon, have always sensed this, this feeling that Jesus was different and was called to a life none of us would understand. So now you all know what only your father and I knew. Your brother belonged to *Adonai*."

James finally says, "I know it now too, Mother."

The others look at each other in silence, drinking in this incredible bit of family history. Maryam goes on to tell them of the birth in Bethlehem, the angels and the shepherds, the Magi, the flight to Egypt, and the alarming prophecies at Jesus' reception at the Temple. Now they all know the remarkable family history.

"But," Maryam goes on, "I know not why, but this morning my heart is light. I keep hearing the sound of your brother's laugh, but I do not think I've gone mad."

Ana puts her hand on her mother's shoulder. "Mama, you saw things last Friday that no mother should ever see. Your heart will feel many strange things for some time to come."

"Yes, my daughter, perhaps you're right. But I don't feel sad anymore."

Just then there is a commotion at the door. Three of the men are trying to shush whoever is there. Finally, they open it and the women come back in, all of them with their eyes large and surprise written on their face. Maryam of Cleopas breathlessly recounts, "We found the stone rolled away and the tomb empty. Maryam of Magdala stayed behind and we began to return here in sadness. We came to tell you."

Petros and Johanan are out the door in a flash and the room buzzes with talk.

"Where is Magdala?" Maryam asks, but no one can tell her. It is perhaps an hour before Petros and Johanan return. "The tomb is empty," Petros tells everyone. "I don't know what it means." Then Sweet Magdala, whom Maryam has come to love, dashes in the door behind Johanan.

"Johanan, Petros! I have seen the Lord! The Master is alive! He spoke to me. He told me to tell you!"[2]

There is a long silence followed by debate. Taoma and Petros are insisting that the women are hysterical. Johanan and his brother Jacob are joyful and saying that the women have seen truly.

But in the far corner Maryam hears her son's laugh and she says to her daughter and two sons sitting by her. "Your brother is no longer dead."

"Mama, we don't know . . .," Ana begins, but Maryam knows in her heart as sure as she knows anything.

"Your brother is alive. I know it."

Shimon interrupts, "I do too. I don't know why, but I can feel it so."

"As can I," James says in self-amazement.

Ana stops and says, "Yes, I feel him too."

Maryam says, "Bring Magdala to me."

Ana goes and brings Magdala over from where she is sitting sadly by herself, hurt not to be believed. Maryam hugs her and gets her to tell them

---

2. John 20: 18,19

all about the empty tomb and the strange bright men they saw. "I stayed behind the others and could not stop my tears. But I saw a man. I thought he was the gardener. He said to me, 'Woman, why are you weeping? Whom are you seeking?' And I thought maybe he had taken my Lord's body, so I told him, 'Sir, if you have carried him off, tell me where you put him and I will get him.' Then he said my name and I recognized him. I held him so tightly, I am sorry, but I had to embrace him. He lives. Mother Maryam, your son lives. I have seen him."

The long quiet day locked away settles down. Magdala and Johanan and his brother Jacob and some of the twelve gravitate to Maryam's side of the room, where their exuberance spills over onto each other. Petros and Taoma and the rest of the men watch the door and sadly shake their heads at their friends. Food is running short. Taoma volunteers to run the risk of going to the market. The door is opened and he is let out. It is shut tight and locked behind him.

After long, quiet hours, evening comes on and Maryam suddenly stands up. Chills course through her and her sleepiness vanishes, replaced by an almost electric sense of joy. She can feel him. "Jesus!" she whispers and suddenly a moment later, Jesus is standing in the middle of the room. Everyone is shocked but Maryam, who plunges toward him with a cry and embraces him, followed by Magdala and Ana.

When calm resumes, Jesus talks to all his followers. Receive the Holy Spirit. The sins you forgive in my name are forgiven. And there was more. Maryam sits at her son's feet, refusing to move further away, though others press near. Her heart swims in joy and peace. *Adonai* did not fail her. He beat death itself. She feels almost like laughing.

And then he's gone, just like that. Today we'd call it teleporting. Maryam feels a disappointment, but she can also feel him around her. This is a new phase, something no one has ever experienced before. Then Taoma arrives with much bread and some fish. Everyone tells him what they've seen, but he refuses to believe.

The following evening, Jesus is there again, suddenly, without warning. Maryam doesn't rush to him this time. She knows that he will always be with her. She lets others draw close, including Taoma, who falls to his knees and exclaims, "My Lord and my God."

Yes, Maryam thinks. My Lord, my God, my son.

Meditation Thirteen: Another Life

WE KNOW THAT THE young *ecclesia*, the fledgling church, gathered around Maryam and Jesus' brothers, and that Petros, Peter, was a leader. Though she did not speak, Maryam saw the miracle of Pentecost. She stood in the street in Jerusalem, in front of the Temple, where she'd almost lost her Jesus twice, and looked amazed at the sight of the tongues of fire that lit themselves on the heads of these young men who all call her Mother. She heard the multiple languages tumble out of their mouths and felt the awe. She saw the crowd look in astonishment on that small band of followers of the Way, and heard Petros and his eloquent speech that did not come from him. She also saw the little flames on the heads of the women of the Way, on Magdala, and Salome, Susana, and Joanna, and on her own dear Ana, though it was not specially mentioned in the later accounts. But Maryam knew about the invisibility of women.

Her life in the middle of this exciting new community takes on an unfamiliar quality. Though she works with the other women in the home of Joseph of Arimithea, as a long-term guest, this is not the way she'd lived her life till now: up with the sun, making the bread, watching the men go off to the fields or to the workshop. Today we'd say she was living the life of a minor celebrity, the Mother of the Risen Jesus, spoken to reverently, in hushed tones. For the first time in her life, she need not work, for shelter and food are given her and those who do so, count themselves honored that she would accept. This feels odd to Maryam. She is not interested in celebrity; she wants people to pay attention to her son. She was not there when he did a remarkable ascension into the skies. She wishes she could have been. The young men, bless them, told her of it afterwards. Johanan told her that her son said he would return. Every once in a while, Maryam looks up from whatever she's doing and looks at the door, as if Jesus should be standing there. She feels him near her, though she does not see nor hear him. He's there.

It was after that time, her favorite of the young men whom had followed her son, young Johanan, though now no longer young, told her of the time that Jesus went up a small mountain and began to glow as he talked to Moses and Elijah. Johanan tells her that he was not allowed to speak of it at the time, and that he, his brother, and Petros, who were all there, even now do not speak of it.

Maryam says, "My son, you should write these things down."

Johanan thinks about this a while and says, "I will. I will start writing what I remember."

And her young men, her son's followers, preach across Jerusalem and the followers of her son's Way grow. But there is push-back and even some violence. The Sanhedrin loathe them and the Romans eye them warily when they pass in the street. Some of the young men are roughed up in the streets. But the Way continues to grow.

Maryam marvels at her life, which used to follow the rhythm of the crops, or the work at Sepphoris. Now it is meetings, for prayer, and reading of scripture, and people who look at her with awe, and ask her about her son. She feels like some sort of royalty and that thought makes her laugh; she is a farm girl who used to rake out dung and had her first child in a stable. There is so much excitement and energy for a year or two. Then it begins to wane and she sees Ana worrying about the dangers. Ana says that she longs to leave Jerusalem. Shimon and James are fully engrossed in the Way and want to stay in the heart of the action. Let them be. Maryam concedes.

After three years in this life, it all seems somehow wrong. Maryam, at her daughter's urging, finally goes home with Ana to Nazareth. Once back home again, she feels better, working daily in her once-again humble existence. Though she revels in her grandchildren, and the weddings of her grandchildren, and the coming of great-grandchildren, there is no peace. All Israel seems to be divided by her son. Those who follow the Way of her Jesus are close to one another and she finds many of them at her door, reverencing her. These strangers standing in the dust, bowing before her astound her. She is honored but also embarrassed by the attention.

But the majority of the people in the town, people once her friends and neighbors, scorn her as the mother of a madman and a heretic. She can feel the division and the tension.

Three years after she returns, and after her son conquered death, death takes its first revenge. Stephanos, a young man she'd met in Jerusalem, is

MEDITATION THIRTEEN: ANOTHER LIFE

stoned to death on the orders of the Sanhedrin, for preaching the good news about her son. The news reaches her a month later. She grieves for him. Why did the Romans all of a sudden start allowing the Sanhedrin to stone people when they felt the need to try her Jesus before Pilate? The news has traveled at high speed, all the way north to Nazareth, where it becomes the town gossip. Neighbors burn her heart by saying aloud in her hearing that it was a good thing that this blasphemer was killed. Maryam begins to fear for her children. *Adonai* has beat death, but it still surrounds them. The final victory is yet to be.

Then one day, Johanan, now much older and his face lined with wrinkles, his beard beginning to gray, shows up at her door. She knows. She says to him.

"It's time to leave, isn't it?"

Johanan nods. She invites him in and he shares the news with her and Ana. It's dangerous to be in Jerusalem. Any follower of the Way of Jesus should be ready to be killed. Johanan has been sent to the community in Antioch, for his own safety and to provide leadership. But James, her son, has asked Johanan to take his mother and sister with him to safety. Thus, Jesus' words from the cross take meaning. Joseph and Judah are determined to stay in Nazareth, and Shimon is with James in Jerusalem. Two of her daughters have husbands. Many of the Way are being stoned to death, as Stephanos was. Other followers of the Way also are all fleeing north to the safety of Antioch, in Syria, where people call them Χριστιανός , *Christianous*, followers of the *Christos*, the *Mashiach*, or the Anointed One, the Messiah. Her son. Her son. It is safe for *Christianous* in Antioch. James and Petros fear for Maryam's safety. If Herod or the Romans want to kill a high-profile follower of the Way, who better than the mother of Jesus? They want her to leave for her own good. When Johanan finishes his account, Ana says softly, "We will have to leave Israel."

They all three, sitting around the family table in Maryam's kitchen enclosure, feel the weight of those fatal words, like an electric shock running through them. Leave? Leave the Promised Land and the Chosen People? Leave the land fought for by Joshua and David, lost and recovered centuries ago, then lost to the Greeks, then the Romans?

"Israel," Maryam says, "Is wherever Jesus is. And my Jesus is where his people are. We will go with you, Johanan, to Antioch."

The house is sold to Judah and Joseph for whatever coins they had on hand. They will then sell it after Maryam and Ana are gone, and the house that Joseph, dear Joseph, built with his hands, in which Jesus and all her children were raised, will go to strangers. Again, Maryam feels strange at the thought and spends her time wandering around the structure, touching the doorposts and the walls, as if to say goodbye. Yet, she is willing to let go. Her hope in in her Jesus who has defeated death. Houses will come and go.

Maryam is 52 years old as they set out. On the ridge north of town, she stops and turns and looks at Nazareth the last time, holding her walking stick and wearing her blue traveling cloak that Shimon made for her. Some of her gray hair blows out under her cloak that covers her head and shades her eyes. Nazareth is just a dusty, little town on a hillside, looking as if a giant had dropped it accidentally on the uneven slopes. She sees her father's farm, now the farm of Judah and Joseph. She knows she will never see that farm nor her sons again in this world. She said goodbye to them last evening, though they looked perplexed and tried to talk her out of going. They know it's dangerous to stay. But they have the farm. It's their life. And they have wives and children. Though they know their brother is the Messiah, they will make themselves quiet, and not provoke their neighbors. Maryam heard them talk this way, and knew that what they suggested was futile. Simeon promised her a sword, but the sword is dividing up all of Israel. It is not ever again going to be safe here. Maryam sighs, turns her face to the north and the road to Antioch, where Ana and Johanan await her. She puts one foot forward, then another. In a few minutes, Nazareth is gone behind them.

For twenty days they walk together, finding hospitable farms or cheap inns at the end of each day. The days are long and the sun hot, but Maryam is relieved to be out walking. She notices that Johanan and Ana have started to talk much on the road, and that they have become friends, and perhaps even more. She is glad. Ana has given so much and asked so little. She hopes that this may become more.

Late on the twentieth day they arrive on the eastern banks of a large river and follow it north into a Roman city as grand as Jerusalem. It is Antioch. Parts of it ride up on a ridge over town. The part in the river valley beneath the ridge is rather splendid with stone construction, towers and Roman architecture, as well as Greek. The river runs through the city, and creates an island in the middle where the grandest buildings are. Maryam's Greek is poor, but she can make out most of the conversations around them as they walk through the paved and crowded streets. Johanan asks directions and they wend their way through a maze of streets to the rather

MEDITATION THIRTEEN: ANOTHER LIFE

large house of one Stephanos, where they are not only welcomed, but find that they are home.

And a new phase of Maryam's life begins. Like in Jerusalem, she is a minor celebrity. She doesn't really like it, but she is becoming accustomed to it. It was when she realizes that with few exceptions, all these followers of the Way are far younger than she, that she begins to think of them all as her little children. They come to her and find in her someone they can talk to without judgment. And she likes to pray with them. It is this element that reconciles this country woman to life as the Mother of the Lord. She effectively becomes everyone's mother. And she finds a richness in this that she would never have expected.

But her motherhood is gladdened at last in the way that she had hoped. One night Johanan, who is now *episcopoi* here, the overseer, comes to her alone and confesses how highly he regards Ana.

"She is such a good and kind woman. I have rarely met someone like her."

Maryam replies, "She shares her eldest brother's love and empathy," referring to Jesus.

Johanan's eyes open a little wider when Maryam says this. "Yes, I had not thought of it like that, but you are right. I see it. But Maryam, I came to ... " Johanan sputters to a stop, lost for words.

Maryam laughs softly. Johanan's reticence reminds her of her own Joseph when he asked her to marry him. She finishes his sentence. "You came to ask me for Ana's hand."

"Uh, yes. I know you need her but ... "

"What does she say?"

"She wants this also. But I don't wish to take her from you, Mother Maryam."

"She will be where you are, Johanan, and I will also. My son has ordered that for you and I. It is a good thing, and I approve with all my heart."

So Johanan and Ana are married. The wedding is different, as the synagogue is hostile. One of the elders, the *presbyters*, speaks the words of commitment and blesses the union in the name of Christ. Maryam marvels at seeing her son now as the one before whom marriage vows are given; but he was not just any son. She still feels his presence all around, especially when they have what we today would call communion services, where they eat the bread and drink the wine. These, and the agape feasts are dear to Maryam's heart. And it is well that her life is granting her more ease. Here hands are starting to become gnarled like old tree roots, and her joints are becoming painful.

In case anyone has a problem with my portrayal of the Apostle John marrying Mary's daughter, let me mention two things: one, it would explain a lot why she went with him when at very least there were cousins out there who could take care of her, even if you don't believe she had any other children. And two, if you're having a problem with this, it may have something to do with the idea that the Apostles were holy, and therefore celibate. There again, we confuse holiness with sexlessness. I've often noticed people jar a little when they read of Jesus healing Peter's mother-in-law.[1] Peter had a wife? We assume the Twelve went around as celibate holy men. But if we do that, we're projecting our Gnostic notions on both history and faith.

Oddly though, in spite of her own mounting ailments of old age, when one of the "children" as she thinks of the followers of the Way, when one comes to her and asks for healing prayers, Maryam gladly prays over them, and quite often they are miraculously healed. Maryam knows that she has healed nobody; once again, it is her son listening to her who heals, though she cannot see him. She always feels him there.

So the years fly by. Sunrise, sunset. Maryam is now clearly an old woman, white-haired, a little stooped and arthritic. But the fire is still in her eyes and she still can walk many miles. Shimon appears one year. His wife is dead. Joseph and Judah were burned out of their farm because it had become a meeting place for the people of the Way in Nazareth. He doesn't know where they've gone. He was hoping to find them here. Maryam talks him into staying with them. He is sad and needs healing. He will find it in the *ecclesia* at Antioch.

After about five years, a Jew that Maryam has heard much of, Shaul of Tarsus, called by the Latin name, Paulus, arrives. Maryam is intrigued with him. He is a small, lanky, intense man, with short, dark hair, a trimmed black beard, and penetrating dark eyes. She senses his intelligence and his compassion. She likes him. He was once a persecutor of the Way but now the Twelve have sent him to minister to the Gentiles in the Greek lands. He asks her many questions about her son, and she answers as best she can. She asks him questions about the Greek lands and is intrigued. And Paulus and Shimon have long talks, for like Shimon, Paulus grieves for the resistance of Israel to the Way of Jesus. Maryam often finds him staring out the door, and he knows that he is reaching out in his heart to his brothers and sisters,

---

1. Matthew 8:14-15, Mark 1:29-31, and Luke 4:38-41

now lost to them: Joseph, Judah, Elisheva, Dvorah and their families. Many Jews have fled to the Greek lands to escape the escalating tensions in Israel. Perhaps they are here somewhere.

Sunrise, sunset. Time passes quickly now.

Petros arrives five years after that. Johanan is glad to see him and asks him to take over being *episcopoi*. For the *ecclesia* at Antioch has become greater than the one in Jerusalem and has sent out not only Paulus, but Barnabbas, Silas, and young Johanan Marcus. Johanan ben Zebediah spends much time talking with Shimon and they both look out the front door from the house on the hill far to the west. They talk with Paulus and Silas about cities to the west where Jews have fled. Maryam can feel Johanan's spirit in restlessness. He wants to follow the Spirit out to the Greek lands and tell them about the Messiah there. Maryam thinks about it. Here in Antioch, over half of them are Jews. Where they go from here, everyone will be a Greek or maybe a Roman. What few Jews they encounter will most likely be hostile. But, like Shimon, she would like to find her scattered sons and daughters if possible. She contemplates this for some days, but her spirit is yearning to see a newer world still, in spite of her aging body. She was even a little envious when they bade Paulus farewell as he headed deep into the Greek lands. Johanan had questioned him closely about the followers of the Way in the cities to the west and had taken thorough notes.

Maryam feels her spirit ache to go. She is still what we'd call today a spunky old lady. She will go. She is 62, still an active walker in spite of the stiffness in her hands. She tells Johanan, who is quite gray-haired himself, and he is content, as is Ana. The three of them will go, though Ana insists that they take a donkey for Maryam in spite of her protests. Shimon says he cannot be parted again from his mother and he wishes to look for his brothers and sisters. He is eager to go. Maryam is glad. The four of them will go.

They set out to the west. After two weeks on the dusty road, they stop at Derbe, where Paulus has founded a community of the Way, an *ecclesia*. They rest two nights and move on to Iconium, there again finding a community established by Paulus. Then there is a long walk of over two weeks to Antioch in Asia, a city with the same name as the one from whence they came, with a community founded by Paulus. Till now, Paulus has paved the way for them. But Johanan and Shimon feel that they need to go back to the coast, for there they will find little Jewish communities and maybe their kin. The people of the Way in this western Antioch show them the road west to the coast. They tell them that it leads to a small coast town known as Ephesus, a great temple city for the goddess Artemis. The four agree and with ample provisions lovingly provided by the *ecclesia* of Antioch, they begin their journey west. They pass through rolling hills of dry brush with a few small trees, though Maryam thinks it is greener and more lush than Israel. It is almost three weeks of journeying, and many times they slept by the side of the road. The rain wet them, but Maryam doesn't care. She feels like she is going forward to where her Jesus awaits her, always in front of her, beckoning her on.

They finally find themselves descending through thick brush and rolling hills into a shallow canyon. Ahead, they smell the sea. They see its blue band spread between the U shape of the break in the hills ahead of them and the road from the town to the harbor. In the canyons to their left, the gleaming marble towers of the city of Ephesus shine in the sunlight. They've been traveling a month and a half. On entering the city, they find no one familiar. The columns and triangle roofs of Greek architecture grace the tall, white buildings.

Johanan, whose Greek is best, starts asking passers by where the *Ioudious* meet. The first people have no idea. They don't even seem to be aware that there are Jews in the Greek lands. However, one merchant at the produce market points out a small building up a back street. They soon find a synagogue and introduce themselves. They ask after Jews coming through the region. Shimon is disappointed to hear that there is no news of their kin. Johanan calmly explains that they are people of the Way, and believers that Jesus of Nazareth was the Messiah. He does not mention that Maryam is Jesus' mother. As everyone expected, most of the people of the synagogue take offense and ask them to leave; their kin in Israel have sent them word about this crazy new sect and they wish to have nothing to do with such Jews. But Tychicus, a Greek convert to Judaism, and his two sisters, Nephele and Selene, follow them out of the building and befriend them. They want to hear more about Jesus of Nazareth. These women take them into their home and an *ecclesia* is born in Ephesus. Maryam and her children live quietly, for the tradesmen of the town are devoted to the Temple of Artemis, and are intolerant of other religions, but still the numbers of the *ecclesia* grow steadily. Maryam finds after a while that the town reminds her too much of Sepphoris and the memory is painful. Johanan and Ana find a small house up a canyon to the south, in a lovely thicket of trees, and buy it with their small stock of money. As Maryam moves in, she knows in her heart that this will be her home until Jesus comes for her.

MEDITATION THIRTEEN: ANOTHER LIFE

But Shimon is restless. Maryam tells him to go look for his brothers and sisters and return if he can. She blesses him, and he goes. But she feels that she may never see him again. She has Johanan and Ana. It is enough. And the *ecclesia* that gathers round them find that her prayers for healing and help are powerful. They come to her quietly, in ones and twos and she prays over them. Sometimes her Jesus grants her prayers and the seekers are healed. She calls them "little children" to their faces, a habit that Johanan picks up.

While there, at Maryam's urging, Johanan begins to pull together his notes and to write the story of Jesus.

Sunrise, sunset.

After 5 years, Paulus and a middle-aged Greek in his 30s, named Lucas come by. Maryam learns that Lucas is a physician. He is writing down the story of the people of the Way. Lucas becomes very attached to Maryam and spends many hours asking her questions. She tells him all the family stories of birth of Jesus, the flight to Egypt, the strange events when he was presented at the Temple, and the time they lost him in the Temple. She has never told anyone outside the family these stories, but she knows her time is passing and the stories must be told. Meanwhile, Paulus speaks in Ephesus and causes a riot that almost gets him killed. He and Lucas have to move on. But as a result of the ruckus Paulus made, the *ecclesia* grows rapidly, and Maryam has many little children to pray for. Things grow quiet again and the little *ecclesia* meets in the home of Nephele and Selene, but they come for prayers to the house of Maryam, Mother of the Lord, up the canyon to the south.

Sunrise, sunset.

Eight years pass. Maryam is 75 and ancient by the standards of the day. Her age alone make her the subject of talk in the city. Nobody lives to 75. She must have some kind of magic or way with the gods. She hears stories of the exaggeration of her age. Some say she is 200 or more. These things make Maryam laugh if she hears them.

She does not leave her house now and can barely walk. Still, the little children of the Way come to her for prayers and quiet miracles occur. She talks to Jesus all the time, though he does not speak back to her in the normal sense. As she grows older, she can feel him everywhere, so she simply speaks out to the seemingly vacant air. She tries not to do it when others are present, lest they think her mad. Though she does not fear to speak to Jesus when Ana is there. Ana has grown old herself, and she and Johanan never had children.

But Ana is happy to be where she is. Maryam is content in all but one thing: she knows nothing of her family outside of Ephesus.

Finally, she says aloud to Jesus in the calm quiet air of her house. "Son, could you send me word about your brothers and sisters? Thank you."

A week later, Shimon shows up. Maryam does not recognize him right away. When he departed, he was still a young man. Now he is aged and his beard begins to turn gray. Sadness is written in his eyes. Of Elisheva and Dvorah, he only learned that they had gone to the Greek lands, though he searched every city, he could not find them. James was stoned to death by the reactionary forces in Jerusalem. Maryam's heart bleeds. It is the final thrust of the sword. Two sons killed, and yet the first conquered death. She says, "We will see James again." Shimon continues. Judah and Joseph managed to finally reach Antioch in Syria, where Maryam and the others used to live, and Judah and Joseph and their families are safe there. Maryam nods. She knows that she cannot journey to see any of them now. Her body is failing her and her next journey will be out of this life. She tells Shimon, "I will not be with you all much longer. Stay with me, my son, till I go to your brother." Shimon nods in assent.

Four years later, Maryam's health fails rapidly with multiple symptoms. She does not leave her bed and Ana rarely leaves her side. Shimon hears news. He tells her that word has come that a revolt has broken out in Israel and the Roman are destroying it. Nazareth has been laid waste, a smoldering ruin. Those Jews that survive are being driven out of Israel. A large force of Jews is making ready for a last stand against the Romans in Judea, at a place called Massada, but there is no hope of success.

"Your brother foretold this," she whispers, as talking is difficult to her. "They could have listened to him and it would have been different." Maryam's mind becomes foggy. There are moments when she recognizes Ana, or Johanan, or Shimon by her bedside. Most of the time, she is a little girl watching sheep in the ravines around Nazareth, or she is helping Joseph to ask her to marry him. There is no particular order to these visions and they seem as real as when she wakes and sees Ana by her bedside. But the moments of clarity do not last and she is in Egypt, protecting her first-born son, or experiencing the agony of giving birth to him in Uncle Levi's stable in Bethlehem. Time seems to have unraveled like an old cloak, and the stray threads are falling everywhere and with no pattern. At one point she hears Shimon say clearly, "Who would have thought that she would live 79 years?"

MEDITATION THIRTEEN: ANOTHER LIFE

Have I really lived 79 years? And I always thought I'd be a simple farm-wife in Nazareth. No, that is not what *Adonai* had in mind for me.

The Catholic Church believes that Mary was assumed into Heaven, body and soul,, after dying. The Orthodox speak of the Dormition, that after being dead 40 days, Mary went body and soul into Heaven. The precedent is Enoch in Genesis 5:21-24, who is taken up by God because he is beloved. I do not know. I resist the idea of Mary as a goddess who avoided suffering, but the miraculous always has surrounded her. I would not be surprised that such a thing had happened. And more importantly, in taking up Maryam body and soul, God confirms that he doesn't disdain flesh-and-blood, like the Gnostics and Manichees believe.

At one point, Maryam's mind clears. All the pain in her body vanishes and she finds herself in bright light which blinds her. She puts up her hands in front of her eyes. As her eyes adjust, she sees that she is standing by a shallow stream. There are trees and grass on the other side; it looks inviting. A riot of birds are singing in joy. The morning sun just peeps over a far ridge, sending soft, warm light over everything. She hears Jesus' voice distinctly now, from the trees across the stream, not far at all.

"Mother. Come."

She looks at her arms and body. She cannot see her face, but her body is like that when she was fifteen and her hands are young and smooth. How can this be? And she is wearing Shimon's blue cloak. She laughs and splashes barefoot across the stream and rounds the first tree-trunk. Jesus is standing there. She does not even pause a moment and is in his arms. And then she has a series of remarkable experiences, which I have no power to narrate. Catholics tell us that she was made Queen of Heaven. But I think for Maryam, just to be with her son would have been worth far more than to be queen of anything.

Back in the 1960s the Soviets mocked the idea of Heaven being in the sky when their cosmonauts circled the earth and did not see it. C.S. Lewis in "The Seeing Eye" points out that one sees what one is prepared to see. I have always wondered if Jesus' ascension was something like interdimensional travel or something else that our physics has yet to sense. Only God knows.

But what is more remarkable than any of that is this: the story isn't over.

Meditation Fourteen: Somewhere Over the Rainbow

THIS IS GOING TO be the hardest chapter I will try to write. We all one day splash across that stream, to the "undiscovered country from whose bourne no traveler returns." Sure, we have small clues from people who have died briefly and been sent back, but as Shakespeare wrote, for the most part it is the ultimate mystery. Our entire trust is in Christ's promise of many mansions.[1] However, the partition is thin for Christians who believe in the Communion of Saints, that is the dead in Christ, who are not really after all, dead, can pray for us and can hear our requests for prayer through the medium of the Holy Spirit.

I can only write about this Earth. I have not yet crossed the bourne of the undiscovered country, and I cannot promise to send word back when I do. But that's just the odd and interesting thing. There have been miraculous answers to prayers that were the result of asking the saints to pray for us. But for the most part, those saints are never seen again on this side of the stream—except Mary. *National Geographic* magazine recently did a story on Mary which included a map of every place she has been known to appear. The dots covered every continent in the world. She has been busy. Boy, has she been busy. But at first it was not so. And I wonder about this. God waits for us to call to him generally. I think Mary, Mother Maryam does the same.

Her first appearance doesn't come for a while. The Gnostics were very taken with her and about 70 or so years after her Assumption into Heaven, one of them writes the fantastic and strange *Protevangelium of James* referred to earlier, in which she is a pain-free goddess, floating serenely above the pain, dirt, and fleshly existence on earth. Most early Christian writers in the early centuries, if they mention her at all, discuss her theologically, as the new Eve. There is a reticence amongst Church leadership to make much of

---

1. John 14:2

her, for fear that she would be merged in the popular mind with Isis or other pagan, virgin goddesses. And in light of the Gnostic version of Mary as the pain-free, serene goddess, I think their fears were justified.

I believe that the Gnostic and Manichaee tendencies were very strong in that cultural soup of the first three centuries of the Roman Empire era church. After all, though the Jews had no concept of virgin goddesses like Artemis/Diana and Athene, nor communities of dedicated Vestal Virgins, the Greeks and Romans certainly did. Spiritual celibacy was a concept in the Roman Empire before Christ. And as of St Anthony's going into the desert around 285, and the movement that eventually became monasticism, celibacy became associated in the Christian community with purity. The idea that the Mother of God would be subsequently touched by a mortal man like Joseph was simply unthinkable to people who had worshiped Artemis and Athene. So the Gnostic disdain of human flesh shouldn't come as a surprise to us.

By the time we get to the late 300s and 400s, church fathers like Gregory of Nyssa are writing about Mary's perpetual virginity as the stop against death, and other symbolic and deep spiritual interpretations. Virginity has become a spiritual super-power, so everyone is convinced that Mary must have had it. The Gnostic and Manichaee concepts, condemned by the church, leech back into Christian thinking. The result is a Mary who is a super-woman, a virtual goddess, and one that causes Protestants to turn away. As I have tried to show, it is just possible that Mary had holiness, intervenes in our lives, but still was a mortal woman who experienced pain and sorrow and was capable of a normal sexual relationship with her husband. In other words, her life was not that far different than ours. I believe we need to realize that if she's not just going to be a glowing figure on the wall that nearly half of Christianity rejects.

For Gnostics and Manichaees, and for many early orthodox Christians, sadly, God was out there and holy beyond any ability we might have to come close to him. Anything associated with God had to also be pure, and spotless, and free from the experience of human flesh with death, disease, and sex and other messy stuff. This is why though the church dismissed the *Protevangelium of James*, later Christians embraced it and embrace it still. Many of us want the Virgin Mary to be super-virgin, untouched by pain and sex and death and normal childbirth. That is what we think holiness looks like—something beyond human experience.

This was the whole problem with the alternate forms of Christianity that emerged in those early centuries. Though many of these forms were declared heresies, their concepts were never entirely cleansed from the mind of the Church, and are still lingering with us. Docetism taught that Jesus was a god and only visually appeared in human flesh, like a hologram. The Gnostics liked the Docetist teachings because it kept Jesus and his mother from being sullied by all that disgusting and dirty human flesh. On the other hand, the Arians taught that Jesus was just a remarkable man inspired by God. In either case, neither extreme could grasp the idea that the Creator of the universe got down and rolled in the mud of human experience. This is what the formulas of the Nicene Creed were about; God became man while still being God. And though we accept this, we cannot really imagine it. Like the Docetists and the Arians, we want it all one way or the other.

But that runs counter to the whole concept of the Incarnation. If God wanted to show up and not "dirty his fingers", he could have easily done that. Jesus Christ could just have appeared, Poof!, no pregnancy and birth necessary. He wouldn't have to grow up and experience puberty and disappointment and probably small run-ins with disease. He wouldn't have to watch his step-father, Joseph, die. In fact, if we follow this very Docetist line of thinking to the end, the whole business on the cross was an unnecessary dirtying of God's fingers. And he could have snapped his fingers and called for miracles that would have blown the Pharisees and the Sadducees away. Then he could have laughed at Pilate and the Roman legions and walked off without a scratch.

What any clear reading of the Gospel shows is that God chose to get not only his fingers dirty, but every other part of him as well. God chose to lay down and roll freely and at length in the mud slough of human existence. Why should his human mother be spared what he chose for himself? Why should Mary have a painless, teleport birth process? Why should she be free of the "taint" of sex? Many Christians were offended by Dan Brown's novel which held that Christ had a child with Mary Magdalene. Though I wasn't upset with Brown's portrayal, I did feel that Brown in some ways was feeding his own Arian urge to make Christ less important, less significant, just another man. But separate from that issue, if the Son of God, who chose to undergo all the pain, dirt, and agony of human experience, chose also to undergo the trials and tribulations of marriage and parent-hood, how would that have been evil? He did not, and I am sure I don't know why, but I cannot think that the choice would have been evil.

I think the reason this neo-Docetist concept of Mary in claiming for her an ever-virginity bothers me is that not just that it is truthfully inaccurate. More to the point, when we push God into this distant, glowing concept of holiness, we are on a subtle level pushing the possibility of becoming more holy ourselves into the realm of the impossible. If being holy is like the Super-Virgin Mary, hovering above the world in painless detachment, well then, we can hardly be expected to be like that. Whew! We're off the hook. It offers all the condolences of religious devotion without the painful repentance and new life that God asks of us.

But, we can't get away with that dodge. Mary's Son said "You be perfect, as your Father in Heaven is perfect."[2] This is not some untouchable state hovering above us, out of our reach. In the Incarnation, God in the form of Christ reaches down and rolls in the mud of existence with us. And we can rise to his level because he has lowered himself in his vast, incomprehensible humility to our level. There are no barriers; holiness is not virginity. It is living like Jesus and doing what he tells us.[3] Jesus did not choose to marry and be a father, but if he had, he would have done that well too. Mary doesn't have to live like a nun in Joseph's house for fifty years of celibacy to reach holiness.

Sadly, the power of the Docetist urge in the culture of the time was stronger in most cases, so by the time of St Jerome, in the late 300s, early 400s, he and other Christian writers were certain that Mary was a celibate nun all her life in Joseph's house, and that the Greek word for brothers in the Gospels *must really mean* cousins, even though there was another Greek word for cousins. The determined belief that celibacy equaled holiness had set in hard, like cured cement. And the battle with the Arians only made it more firm. But I dare not get too self-righteous here. We all tend to project our cultural concepts on God. It is hard to rise above that.

Cunneen writes of this time:

> From the second century on, small groups of Christian men and women committed to sexual renunciation scattered throughout the eastern Mediterranean as missionaries of celibacy. Filled with a sense that the end of the world was near, they wanted to halt the cycle of procreation and live in a more radical freedom

2. Matthew 5:48
3. John 15:14

by renouncing married life. In 285, Anthony of Egypt, who had earlier given away all his possessions and committed himself to a life of prayerful celibacy, retired completely from "the world" into the desert to achieve a disciplined life of holiness. By 400 CE, some five thousand monks had followed his example, entering the desert on both sides of the Nile, fleeing the worldliness that accompanied the church's collaboration with imperial power.[4]

One can plainly see how this celibacy taken on to achieve a spiritual focus, through typically human sloppy thinking, can turn to the Gnostic conviction that sex is evil and that Christ's mother could never have indulged in that evil. But enough of this. Point made. If someone is not convinced, there is no more to say.

Mary doesn't stay away long. In Ephesus the Cappodocian church father, Gregory of Nazianzus was one of those in the controversy of the nature of Christ. He stood up for the Nicene Creed understanding of Christ being God and man both. At his small church, called the Anastasia, in around 440 many of the faithful came to ask Mary's prayers for their healing, and according to the historian Somozen, they in many cases were healed.[5] This seems fitting to me that in the place where Mary had prayed for the healing for the "little children" of the church at Ephesus, she was still doing so some 400 Earth years after she left us.

As the Gnostic and Arian controversies were finally put to rest, this understanding of Mary as mother of both the human side of Jesus and at the same time, Jesus as the Son of God, gained a spectacular degree of respect for Mary. This is the era of churches springing up, that were named after her, all around the Mediterranean. And with fame, came more requests for prayer to the Mother of God. My thought is that Mary rose to the occasion. And she never really has stopped praying for us, her "little children." Sometimes the results are subtle, as what happened to me. At other times we have something as spectacular as Fatima or Lourdes. The appearance at Tepeyac Hill in Mexico so influenced a culture that the image of Mary as Our Lady of Guadalupe is almost more national than the Mexican flag as a symbol. When I worked as a high school teacher in a Mexican enclave, no year went by without classes full of Marias and Lupes (the common abbreviation of the girls' name Guadalupe), and an occasional Lourdes or Fatima. Over two successive years, two students in my classes were both Maria and sisters to

4. Cuneen, *In Search of Mary*, 107.
5. Cuneen, *In Search of Mary*, 130.

MEDITATION FOURTEEN: SOMEWHERE OVER THE RAINBOW

each other. Their mother apparently was incapable of naming a girl child anything else; only their middle names were different.

But that's us. There is a lot to say about how Mary has influenced culture over the ages. Cunneen's book and others document this thoroughly. What about Mary as a person and not as we see her? At this point my speculative biographical approach breaks down. I do not know what it's like for the dead in Christ. I suspect that they live outside time and gravity (if those two things *are really* two different things), in another dimension. Like C.S. Lewis, I also suspect that the miracles of Jesus such as the walking on the water, and the teleporting, are hints of what the Resurrection body is capable of. But I have not yet crossed that shallow stream.

Still, there are rays of light that break through the wall here and there. Mary's first return to earth is modest. A pupil of Origen, one Gregory, bishop of Neocaesarea, had a vision as a young man in which Mary and the apostle John, (our Maryam and Johanan ben Zebediah) discussed a theological crisis that was raging in Gregory's mind, and set him straight. This was probably a dream, but to my mind, I don't believe it was any less real for that. The date is uncertain, but is probably in the early 200s, two centuries before the healings at the Anastasia church.

Across the centuries there have been other visions, and in fact, we have no way of knowing about appearances that were kept quiet, or how many hundreds or even thousands there might have been. Mary doesn't seem to favor one continent over another, nor any branch of Christianity over another, save where she is resisted. There aren't so many Protestant visitations, but then Protestants generally don't believe that she does visit, and therefore, as with the Russian cosmonauts, even if they saw it, they would explain it away. Catholics are most likely to become enthusiastic about visits, and she has not disappointed this largest branch of Christ's church.

Heaven only knows—and I mean that quite literally—the number and nature of the visits to persons from this point on. I imagine some people had full-on appearances and saw Maryam of Nazareth face to face. Others, like myself, sensed her presence without sight or hearing, and were granted a grace. Others, sadly, convinced themselves Mary spoke to them, and then uttered some nonsense in God's name. There will always be fake revelation so long as there is authentic revelation. Lucifer, if I may say it, is a diligent hacker.

Though the appearance in Mexico in 1531 is perhaps the first major revelation, the real break from the pattern is when Mary appeared to a nun named Catherine Labouré in 1830. Suddenly, and God alone knows why, the pace picks up. Thereafter there are visitations at La Salette in 1846, Lourdes in 1858, Pontmain 1870, Knock in 1879, Fatima in 1917, Beauring in 1932, and Banneux in 1933. And these are only some of the major ones that the Catholic Church backs as authentic because of the ponderous weight of witnesses after thorough investigations.

More important than the fact of notoriety, is that Mary herself here has changed modes. In small revelations, like mine, her goal is to help someone. When she visits Catherine Labouré or Bernadette Soubirous, she has something for them to convey to the world. They are not there to be helped; they are there to carry a message. Mary has set her face yet again.

Three things stand out to me in these messages. First, they are initially almost all to young, and poor girls. All of the recipients are poor, to be sure. Some are nuns, but most not. Juan Diego seems to be almost the sole boy. Mary goes to the least qualified and the least likely to be believed. Just as only Joseph believed her pregnancy was divine, initially no one believed these young people. Second, Mary seeks them out for a specific purpose, to change the course of history. Mary's messages seem to mainly be variations on the theme that if people don't repent and turn to her Son, things are going to get really bad. Many of these appearances are in the 20th century and foretell the forthcoming misery of the world wars. Third, though the so-called major appearances get much attention, Mary's attempts to keep us from destroying ourselves meet with seemingly little success.

A lot of words have been written in the last fifty years or so trying to claw back the concept of an angry Jehovah, an angry God. Frankly, for the most part, Christianity has been embarrassed by the whole angry God thing and we're collectively blushing. We've been shoving that concept behind the couch and emphasizing the God who is love. This was probably a response to the over-doing of the wrath of God by Puritans, both the Protestant and Catholic varieties.

But I find that we err when we try to emphasize one quality of God as found in the scripture as opposed to another. So when we suppress the fact that God is love, we get New England Puritans raging from pulpits, slamming down their Bibles, and promising hell fire, or in the Catholic version that James Joyce found so intolerable, an angry God being held back from throwing lightning bolts by the weeping intercessions of the Virgin Mary. But we fail to realize that God can both be love and be angry. Like the Docetists and the Arians, we make the mistake of thinking that God has to be all one thing or another. We have no sense of balance. Yes, God is love. We weren't wrong about that. He also has every right to be angry.

Of course, this makes some people bristle, this angry Jehovah, which in many cases is the reason why they turned their backs on Christianity. But it depends. It depends on what you perceive God to have been angry about. If you think that God is mad at us for having a good time and enjoying love, well, that sort of angry Jehovah I couldn't believe in either. But can you believe in a God who hates racism and genocide? Can you believe in a God who hates cruelty? Can you believe in a God who was infuriated by the Holocaust? Can you believe in a God who hates arrogance and the wealthy taking advantage of the poor? Can you believe in a God that is angered by rape and murder and human trafficking? Can you believe in a God who hates hate, who hates cruelty and xenophobia? I think God has every right to be thoroughly pissed off about human behavior. We seem to have forgotten that we are sinners, though we howl at the sins, as if some other race had done them. Or we try to explain them away with some tweaked version of psychology.

Another thing that strikes me about all these visitations is the effect they have. We respond to Mary in a way different from the way we respond to God. And for some, that opening of the door in responding to Mary is the only way to move forward toward God. Cunneen talks at length and very insightfully about Mary as the feminine approach to God This is not to say that Mary is the fourth person in the Trinity, as so many Protestants fear that Catholics believe. Nor is it to say that Mary is the feminine softening influence on an angry Jehovah. But human beings are complex creatures psychologically. And some of us respond better to the feminine. This is why there were pagan goddesses and why in many places, upon the arrival of Christianity, worship of some goddess was quickly and easily converted to veneration for the Virgin Mary. And this goes a long way to explain the thick crowds that daily descend upon Marian sites like Lourdes and Fatima.

So what is there left to say? Mary won't leave us alone. The love of God so fills her now in that far dimension that she keeps coming back here trying to keep us from going off the rails. She visits little shepherd girls and a shepherd boy, as she was once a shepherd girl. She even stoops to pay a subtle visit to someone like me, believe it or not. I am still amazed. But all of what she is in that far dimension, that undiscovered country, is the sum of what she once was on the dusty streets of Nazareth, and as she screamed in pain while giving birth in a donkey stall in Bethlehem. She is one tough lady, whose empathy and heart are infused with grace and love beyond our comprehension. Since she told Catherine and Bernadette that she was the Immaculate Conception, I'll just take her word for it. It would explain a lot.

Holy Mary, Mother of God, pray for us fools, us haters, us arrogant jerks, us selfish dolts, us seething racists, us greedy hoarders, us . . . sinners, now and in the hour of our death.

And thanks, Mother. We don't deserve you.

Bibliography

Asch, Sholem. *Mary*. New York: Putnam, 1949.
Campiotti, Giacomo, dir. *Mary of Nazareth*. Tunisia: Lux Vide, 2012.
Chadwick, Henry. *The Early Church*. New York: Penguin, 1993.
Cunneen, Sally. *In Search of Mary: the Woman and the Symbol*. New York: Ballantine, 1996.
"Did the Herodian Temple Have Virgins?" christianity.stackexchange.com/questions/39642/did-the-herodian-temple-have-virgins.
Emmerich, Anne Catherine. *The Life of the Blessed Virgin Mary: From the Visions of Ven. Anne Catherine Emmerich*. Translated by Michael Palairet. Charlotte: Tan, 2004.
Eusebius. *The History of the Church*. Translated by G. A. Williamson. New York: Penguin, 1969.
Hahn, Scott. *Hail, Holy Queen: The Mother of God in the Word of God*. New York: Doubleday, 2001.
Hazleton, Lesley. *Mary: A Flesh-and-Blood Biography of the Virgin Mother*. New York: Bloomsbury, 2004.
"The Infancy Gospel of James." https://www.asu.edu/courses/rel376/total-readings/james.pdf.
Jurgens, William A., trans. *The Faith of the Early Fathers, Volume 1*. Collegeville: Liturgical, 1979.
———. *The Faith of the Early Fathers, Volume 2*. Collegeville: Liturgical Press, 1979.
———. *The Faith of the Early Fathers, Volume 3*. Collegeville: Liturgical Press, 1979.
Korb, Scott. *Life in Year One: What the World was Like in First-Century Palestine*. New York: Riverhead, 2010.
Lacuna, Alveus. "Presentation of the Theotokos and Jewish Temple Virgins." http://www.orthodoxchristianity.net/forum/index.php?topic=23871.0.
Levy, Daniel S. *The Story of Mary: from Biblical World to Today*. Washington, DC: National Geographic, 2018.
Lewis, C. S. "The Efficacy of Prayer." *The World's Last Night and Other Essays*. San Diego: Harcourt, 1960.
Longenecker, Dwight. "The Temple and the Garden of God." *Standing on My Head* (blog), November 27, 2012. https://www.patheos.com/blogs/standingonmyhead/2012/11/the-temple-and-the-garden-of-god.html.
Molnar, Michael R. *The Star of Bethlehem: The Legacy of the Magi*. New Brunswick: Rutgers University Press, 1999.
Nutzman, Megan. "Mary in the *Protevangelium of James*: A Jewish Woman in the Temple?" *Greek, Roman, and Byzantine Studies* 53 (2013) 551–78. https://grbs.library.duke.edu/article/viewFile/14673/3895.

BIBLIOGRAPHY

Rudd, Steve. "Marriage in the Bible and Ancient Marriage and Jewish Wedding Customs: The Three Stage Ritual of Bible Marriages." http://www.bible.ca/marriage/ancient-jewish-three-stage-weddings-and-marriage-customs-ceremony-in-the-bible.htm.

Shoemaker, Stephen J. trans. *The Life of the Virgin by Maximus the Confessor*. New Haven: Yale University Press, 2012.

Tillich, Paul. *A History of Christian Thought*. New York: Touchstone, 1972.

www.ingramcontent.com/pod-product-compliance
Lightning Source LLC
Chambersburg PA
CBHW070922160426
43193CB00011B/1558